Bequest to the Na

A Play

Terence Rattigan

Samuel French – London
New York – Sydney – Toronto – Hollywood

A BEQUEST TO THE NATION

This play was presented at the Theatre Royal, Haymarket, London on September 23rd, 1970 with the following cast:

GEORGE MATCHAM SNR	Ewan Roberts
KATHERINE MATCHAM	Jean Harvey
BETSY	Deborah Watling
GEORGE MATCHAM JNR	Michael Wardle
EMILY	Una Brandon-Jones
FRANCES, LADY NELSON	Leueen MacGrath
NELSON	Ian Holm
LORD BARHAM	A.J. Brown
EMMA HAMILTON	Zoe Caldwell
FRANCESCA	Marisa Merlini
LORD MINTO	Michael Aldridge
CAPTAIN HARDY	Brian Glover
REV WILLIAM NELSON	Geoffrey Edwards
SARAH NELSON	Eira Griffiths
HORATIO	Stuart Knee
CAPTAIN BLACKWOOD	Geoffrey Beevers
FOOTMEN, MAIDS	Stanley Lloyd
	Conrad Asquith
	Graham Edwards
	Chris Carbis
	Deborah Watling

Directed by	PETER GLENVILLE
Settings designed by	OLIVER SMITH
Costumes by	BEATRICE DAWSON
Lighting by	JOE DAVIS

ACT ONE
Scene One   The Matchams' house in Bath
Scene Two   The Admiralty
Scene Three Emma Hamilton's house in Clarges Street
Scene Four   Lady Nelson's house in Somerset Street

ACT TWO
Nelson's house at Merton

The main action of the play covers the twenty-five days between Nelson's return to England on August 20th and his departure for Cadiz on September 13th, 1805. The 'Naval Action fought off Cape Trafalgar' was on October 21st of that year, and the final scene of the play would have taken place some days after the news reached London, on November 5th.

BEQUEST TO THE NATION *

ACT ONE

Scene One

The scene is set on L. side of stage and shows the MATCHAMS'
drawing-room at Bath.   MATCHAM is seated at the table D. L. reading
a newspaper.   There is a tray with coffee pot and cups on the table.
Two menservants are carrying a trunk off R. C. BETSY comes down
the stairs carrying a hat box and KATHERINE's travelling coat.   She is
followed by KATHERINE.

KATHERINE	Betsy - Betsy. My jewel case please. It's in that hat box.
BETSY	Very well, ma'am.
KATHERINE	(joining MATCHAM at the table) Is that today's Chronicle?
MATCHAM	A special edition. Look - the whole front page.
KATHERINE	That was to be expected.
BETSY	Here it is, ma'am. (She crosses to KATHERINE

*N.B. Paragraph 3 on page ii of this Acting Edition regarding photocopying and
video-recording should be carefully read.

with box, hands it to her and places coat on bench
U. L.)

KATHERINE   The trunk is on the carriage?

BETSY   Tom's putting it on now, ma'am.   (She goes out.)

KATHERINE   How long have we?

MATCHAM   The coach goes in half an hour. We should leave in
about ten minutes.

KATHERINE   Is there anything in about us?   (She sits on bench
U. L. placing hat box beside her.)

MATCHAM   (reading)   'Despite the suddenness of Lord
Nelson's return to England it appears that he has
already invited many of his family and friends to
visit him at his house at Merton. Among residents of
Bath so honoured are his sister Katherine and her
husband, Mr George Matcham, the well-known
financier - '

KATHERINE   Financier I never cared for. It sounds - it sounds as
if -

MATCHAM   I dealt in finance. I do.

KATHERINE   But as if you did so as a business.

MATCHAM   I do so as a business.

KATHERINE   But not as a businessman, dear. That is what
always sounds so unrefined.

MATCHAM   Then I am unrefined.   (Rising and moving U. S.)
There seems to be this growing assumption that
since your brother has become a demi-god you have
become a demi-goddess, and that you have therefore
married quite beneath you.   (Crossing to above
table.)   When you were at Burnham Rectory you
were quite glad enough to land a businessman,
Madam.

KATHERINE   There is no need to get in a pother, or to shout.
What else does it say about us?

MATCHAM	Nothing more about us. Something about young George joining us at Merton next week when his college term ends.
KATHERINE	I rather wish they had not mentioned that.
MATCHAM	˙Why?
KATHERINE	People might think it - well - not quite suitable. I mean in the circumstances.
MATCHAM	Why should it be less suitable for George to visit Merton than for us?
KATHERINE	You know perfectly well what I mean.
MATCHAM	Our son is no longer a child, Madam.
KATHERINE	He may not be a child, dear, but his knowledge of the world is extremely limited.
MATCHAM	Yes, and it is high time it was enlarged. (Sits R. of table.)
KATHERINE	(crossing U. S.) Is there much there about our dear Emma?
MATCHAM	Very much.
KATHERINE	Nothing I trust out of place?
MATCHAM	Dammit, Madam, what, in this case, is in place?
KATHERINE	If it is written with delicacy -
MATCHAM	It sounds far worse. Here we have her flitting about between her house in Clarges Street and her temporary abode at Merton -
KATHERINE	Temporary is perfectly delicate.
MATCHAM	And how delicate is this? 'Temporary abode at Merton, where she will no doubt be pleased to enact that role of honorary hostess to the House of Nelson which befits her Ladyship as gracefully in her widowhood as ever it did in former times when her husband, Sir William, Lord Nelson and Her Ladyship were all three joined together in bonds of perfect amity - tria juncta in uno - three joined in one. '

KATHERINE   (coming down to table)   I have explained that situation to George.

MATCHAM   I am sure that your explanation was a model of refinement and sensibility. What was it?

KATHERINE   Well, I told him that the romantic and high-minded friendship of three spiritual and superior human beings, was not to be judged by the coarse standards of common morality.   (She sits on chair L of table.)

MATCHAM   Did you indeed?

KATHERINE   And he believed me, too.

MATCHAM   In that case his knowledge of the world is in for a dazzling enlargement. And if he believes that about the past what exactly does he believe about the present?

KATHERINE   The same, I'm sure.

MATCHAM   The romantic and high-minded friendship of two spiritual and superior beings?

KATHERINE   I think so. Of course I can't be sure. Well, you know how he simply worships his uncle, and so, of course, he should. Pour me some more coffee, dear.

                   (GEORGE appears on stairs carrying books.)

GEORGE   Won't you miss the coach?

MATCHAM   No. We have time.

GEORGE   It would be awful if you did miss it.   (Puts books on bench.)

KATHERINE   Did I hear you walking about last night, dear?

GEORGE   Yes, I couldn't sleep.   (Moves to above table.)

KATHERINE   Excitement?

GEORGE   I suppose so.   (Kisses KATHERINE.)   I wish I could come with you. A week is an awfully long time to wait.

KATHERINE   Will you be nervous arriving at Clarges Street all on
                 your own?

GEORGE   Oh yes, of course. I'm always nervous of him any-
                 way and I haven't seen him for three years nearly. I
                 know he's the gentlest and kindest man alive, but
                 well - he is Nelson.   (Crosses to sit on bench.)
                 As for her - well -   (He hesitates.)

KATHERINE   Well?

GEORGE   The most famous beauty in the world - and loved by
                 him. Of course I'll be nervous. Nervous as Hades.
                 But still, it's a wonderful kind of nervousness to
                 have. I wouldn't be without it.   (He picks up his
                 books.)

                 (BETSY appears with EMILY.)

MATCHAM   Kitty, we should go, I think. Incidentally I have
                 often wondered why, if you possess a jewel case, you
                 should always put it in your hat box.

                 (EMILY has had the courage to enter the morning-
                 room. MATCHAM sees her and starts. Pause.)

                 Why, Emily, what a surprise. How pleasant to see
                 you. How are you, these days?

EMILY   Quite well, thank you, Mr Matcham.   (Bobbing.)
                 Mrs Matcham.

                 (KATHERINE nods.)

                 Why, Master George, how you've grown.

GEORGE   Have I?

EMILY   Oh yes. Quite the young man now.   (To
                 MATCHAM and KATHERINE.)   Lady Nelson's
                 compliments to you both and might she have two
                 words with you. She's waiting outside.

KATHERINE   Outside this house?

EMILY   Yes, Ma'am, in her chaise.

KATHERINE   Well, quite aside from the propriety of that, she has left it rather too late –

EMILY   Just two words, Her Ladyship said. She has read by
                        the papers how you were both going to Merton House
                        today, and she's most anxious to see you.

KATHERINE   You may tell your mistress, Emily, that there is no
                        point whatever in our seeing her at the present time
                        and in the present circumstances, and that she should
                        know much, much better than to ask such a thing at
                        all, and that my husband and I confess ourselves
                        extremely surprised at such unrefined behaviour.
                        You may quote those very words, Emily – in full.

EMILY   Very good, Mrs Matcham. I told her it was no good.
                        I told her not to try –

KATHERINE   She should have listened to you.   (Graciously.)
                        We bear you personally, Emily, no ill-will at all.

EMILY   Very kind, Ma'am, I'm sure.   (She bobs and
                        goes.)

KATHERINE   (outraged)   Well. The insensibility of it! What
                        a cold, hard, conniving bitch! George, you did not
                        hear that.

GEORGE   (grinning)   I did.

KATHERINE   Oh wait till I tell Horatio of this latest exploit of Tom
                        Tit.   (To MATCHAM who has risen to above
                        table.)   Do you know what I think she's going to do
                        now? I think she's going to blockade us in here, so
                        that we can't possibly go to our carriage without
                        passing her chaise and talking.   (Picking up coat
                        and hat box from bench with determination.)   Well,
                        if she thinks that, she's in for a very big surprise.
                        (To MATCHAM.)   Come.   (She crosses to get
                        case.)

MATCHAM   Should we? I confess, I have no great stomach for
                        an armed sortie against an enemy in force.

GEORGE   (grinning)   That from a Nelson.

MATCHAM   Don't be impertinent, sir. And I am not a Nelson.

KATHERINE   Well, I am, and to walk past that chaise and give
             that woman one of my special looks will not dismay
             me at all. I shall, in fact, relish it keenly.   (She
             goes out R.)

MATCHAM   (embracing GEORGE)   Goodbye, George. When I
             see you at Merton in a week's time I expect a good
             report from your Principal.

GEORGE   I hope I'll give you one, sir.

MATCHAM   (benignly – he is fond of his son)   Even if you have
             to write it yourself, eh?   (He goes out R.)

KATHERINE   (off)   We are leaving, Bob.

             (BOB appears, takes travelling bag and hat-box
             from floor near bench and takes them off R.)

MATCHAM   (off)   Kitty, we could easily send Betsy to tell the
             carriage to come to the back door.

KATHERINE   (off, outraged)   The back door? To avoid Tom
             Tit? What kind of man are you?

MATCHAM   (off)   A man civilised enough to wish to avoid
             causing hurt to a member of his family.

             (GEORGE sits at table and opens his books. BETSY
             appears and approaches GEORGE as if she had been
             waiting for this moment.)

BETSY   Oh, Master George, I do envy you.

GEORGE   I'm not surprised, Betsy.

BETSY   Fancy sitting in the same room with him, looking at
             him close. Do you know what I think? You're the
             luckiest young chap in the whole of England.

GEORGE   Well, to be frank, Betsy, I think I am too.

BETSY   I'm going to buy him something and next week you
             can take it down to him and tell him it comes from
             me.

GEORGE   You shouldn't spend your money, Betsy. Why don't
             you just write him a note?

BETSY   A note? To him? Oh no. I don't write that kind of
             English.

             (Bell rings.)

             That's the post. No, I'll think of something to send
             him. Only don't forget to tell him who it comes
             from.

GEORGE   I won't, I promise.

             (BETSY goes. GEORGE goes back to his homework.

             After a moment, BETSY, looking startled, reappears
             - followed by FRANCES, LADY NELSON. She is the
             same age as her husband (46). Her face was never
             beautiful, but it has a composure and a gentle
             dignity that gives it distinction. She walks with a
             stiff gait and uses a stick, but she stands straight.
             BETSY indicates the morning-room, and then flees.)

FRANCES   Good morning, George.

             (GEORGE is deeply alarmed and leaps to his feet,
             but flight is impossible. He gives her, at length, a
             stiff, formal bow.)

GEORGE   Your Ladyship.

FRANCES   (returning the bow)   Am I no longer Aunt Frances?

GEORGE   (bowing again)   Aunt Frances.

FRANCES   Emily was right. You have grown. That jacket is
             far too small for you. Who buys your clothes for
             you now?

GEORGE   My mother.

FRANCES   I did rather better when I used to buy your clothes.
             Kitty never did understand how quickly boys grow out
             of things.

GEORGE   (making a decisive movement)   I must go to my
             class, so, if your Ladyship will forgive me -

FRANCES   (with some edge)   Her Ladyship will not forgive
             you. Nor will your Aunt Frances, who knows

perfectly well what time your classes start. Sit down, George.

(GEORGE involuntarily obeys the voice of authority and sits.)

You are going to Merton next week?

GEORGE   Yes.

FRANCES   On what day?

GEORGE   Thursday.

FRANCES   I am going to London on Tuesday - to my house in Somerset Street. I shall be there several weeks.

(Pause. GEORGE says nothing. There seems, indeed, nothing for him to say. But FRANCES has hoped that he would say something, for she is plainly searching for words, and her brief access of auntly authority has not dissipated her extreme nervousness. She crosses to table.)

Is this coffee still hot?

GEORGE   (starting to rise)   I'll order some more.

FRANCES   (stopping GEORGE and pouring coffee)   This will do. There's an extra cup. It's almost as if they expected me to breakfast. Your mother delivers a cut so badly, George. You should look through your victim, not over her head. And your father - (She laughs, then tries to pull herself together.) Oh George, forgive me. The truth is you make me so nervous that I can't speak -

GEORGE   I make you nervous?

FRANCES   Look at my hand.   (She puts the coffee cup down. It has indeed been impossible for her to get it to her mouth.)   Isn't it silly?

GEORGE   Yes, it is. If you're like this with me, I can't think what you'd have been like with mother and father, if they'd let you come in.

FRANCES   Oh, not nervous at all. It's they whose hands would

have been shaking, not mine. It's guilt makes
people's hands shake, George. Conscience making
cowards of us - like you bowing to the ground and
saying 'Ladyship' to an aunt you used once to call
your favourite.

GEORGE   Why have you a conscience about me?

FRANCES   (crossing to C)   Because of something I'm going to
ask you to do for me - something my conscience says
I shouldn't.

GEORGE   What is it?

FRANCES   Take a letter to Merton.

GEORGE   To him?

FRANCES   To my husband.

(Pause. GEORGE frowns as he tries to think of ways
in which his conscience might be persuaded to say
no.)

GEORGE   What kind of letter?

FRANCES   An ordinary letter.

GEORGE   Does it say anything beastly - like calling Lady
Hamilton a harlot?

FRANCES   It doesn't mention Lady Hamilton. If it did there
would be little point in reminding him of the
profession she is reputed to have once followed.

GEORGE   (angrily)   Are you suggesting that she really was
a harlot?

FRANCES   (smiling)   Of course not, George. I'm merely
observing that in the matter of preserving her
original countrybred chastity, appearances do seem
to have been somewhat against her.   (Sitting on
chair L of table and opening her reticule.)   Now
here is the letter. As you see, the covering is
blank, and I haven't used my seal.

GEORGE   Why?

FRANCES	My handwriting and seal are both well-known to your hostess.
GEORGE	You mean she'd burn it, or something?
FRANCES	No. She would probably do the same thing with it as the last time I sent it four years ago. It was returned to me, and the covering had a message written on it. 'Opened by mistake by Lord Nelson, but not read'.
GEORGE	In her handwriting?
FRANCES	No. Mr Davidson's.
GEORGE	Uncle Horatio's agent?
	(FRANCES nods.)
	She made him do that?
FRANCES	I'm sure of it. Mr Davidson would hardly have done so otherwise.
GEORGE	But Mr Davidson used to be a great friend of yours.
FRANCES	So did a lot of people.
GEORGE	(a shade shame-facedly) Yes, I suppose so.
FRANCES	(affectionately) Dear George, you look so grown up now –
GEORGE	But I can't believe anyone would behave like that. And Mr Davidson – it's such a bad thing to do to Lord Nelson – of all people – to make him seem dishonourable. Look, Aunt Frances – I'm not being rude but you know what people say about you in the family, these days?
FRANCES	About the mischief-making Tom-Tit?
GEORGE	Well, both mother and father say you do make things up about the present situation.
FRANCES	Why do I need to make things up?
GEORGE	Well, to get pity and so on.
FRANCES	I hate pity. I can't bear it.

GEORGE   Well, you can't deny you must feel pretty hostile to
            Lady Hamilton.

FRANCES   No, I can't deny that. But what I told you about that
            letter is true. Read what is written under the cover.
            (She takes the letter out of her reticule and removes
            the outer covering showing him the enclosure.)

GEORGE   'Opened by mistake by Lord Nelson, but not read.
            A. Davidson. '

            (FRANCES nods.)

            It is the same letter?

FRANCES   Yes.

GEORGE   When was it written?

FRANCES   On December eighteenth, 1801.

GEORGE   A Christmas letter?

FRANCES   I hadn't, until now, connected that rejected letter of
            mine with any special season.

GEORGE   (gravely)   You will swear that there's nothing in it
            that will upset him or make him angry?

FRANCES   There is nothing in the letter itself that a wife might
            not write to a husband who has left her   and whom she
            still most deeply loves.

GEORGE   (uncomfortably)   But do you? They all say -

FRANCES   (shortly)   I know what they all say.   (Brightly.)
            Your mother looks well, George. I saw her and your
            father at the Pump Room the other night - together
            with your Uncle William and Aunt Sarah. Quite an
            assembly of in-laws, I must say. Of course I fled.
            Poor things. It is difficult for them all being in Bath.
            In London, of course, things are different. I so
            seldom go out there. Are you going to give him that
            letter?

GEORGE   Yes.

FRANCES   To him personally?

GEORGE   Oh, of course.

FRANCES   You're not scared?

GEORGE   Of him? Of Uncle Horatio? Of course not. He's
              the kindest soul alive.

FRANCES   Yes, he is.   (There is no irony.)   There's not
              a midshipman sails with him who doesn't worship
              him.   (She gets up with difficulty.)   Is that a
              promise, George?

GEORGE   Yes. A promise.

FRANCES   And, of course, you must not tell your mother –

GEORGE   (laughing)   Is that likely?

FRANCES   (crossing to above table and fumbling in her purse)
              I haven't seen you for three Christmases.

GEORGE   Aunt Frances, I don't need bribing.

FRANCES   No. I'm sorry.   (Timidly.)   Of course, if you
              could let slip that I am returned to Somerset Street –
              and would be overjoyed to – set eyes on him again –
              just once, alone, for a few brief moments – no one
              need ever know he'd been to see me – or if he'd just
              give me some inkling where I could go to see him –
              not to talk, George, if it displeases him – or at least
              only about such trivial things as whether his eye still
              hurts him and if he is still wearing his green shade –
              or just if he'd let me sit in a room with him alone,
              not speaking at all, just looking – I'm sorry – I forget
              how I began the sentence. A bad habit.   (Crossing
              D.R.)   You had better tell him none of these
              things. They would only irritate him.   (Brightly
              again.)   Just tell him you were waylaid by Tom
              Tit in your own home and that she gave you that
              letter. Oh, do explain, George, why am I now called
              Tom Tit?

GEORGE   Don't you know?

FRANCES   No.

GEORGE   You won't mind?

FRANCES   Of course not.

GEORGE   It's the way you walk.

FRANCES   The way I walk?

GEORGE   Yes, like a bird.   (Politely.)   At least that's
                 what they say –

FRANCES   Of course. With my rheumaticky legs, it must
                 seem most bird-like. I see.

                 (They are both smiling, GEORGE rather embarras-
                 sedly, FRANCES as if enjoying a joke.)

                 And does Lord Nelson call me that, too?

GEORGE   Oh yes.

FRANCES   You've heard him.

GEORGE   Oh yes.   (Hastily.)   It's not unkind.

FRANCES   No, of course it's not unkind –   (She sits on bench
                 and the tears that have never been far away during
                 the scene now come out in sudden ugly racking sobs.
                 GEORGE crosses to her and stands helpless,
                 watching her.)

GEORGE   Shall I get Emily?

FRANCES   No.

                 (GEORGE watches her unhappily while she struggles
                 to recover herself.)

                 Oh, dear Heavens, I'm so sorry –

GEORGE   (sitting next to her)   I don't understand.

FRANCES   What don't you understand?

GEORGE   What you did to make them all so against you.

FRANCES   What do your mother and father say I did?

GEORGE   They won't tell me, but they're always hinting it was
                 very bad –

FRANCES   Perhaps it was.

GEORGE   What was it?

FRANCES   In the end I told him he had to choose.

GEORGE   But that's not bad.

FRANCES   It was for him.

GEORGE   But is that all?

FRANCES   I think so.

                (She gets up. GEORGE tries to help her.)

                I'm all right now, thank you, George. Perfectly all
                right. Yes, I've often wondered how else I've
                offended.

GEORGE   But why did the whole family turn against you?

FRANCES   (in a hard voice)   Why does your Reverend Uncle
                William now hold a stall at Canterbury, when he
                can't read so much as a Morning Collect? Why is
                your cousin Tom Bolton a Knight before he is even
                twenty? Why is – oh, it doesn't matter. Lord
                Nelson is deservedly a man of great and powerful
                influence in England, and he is very good to his
                family.

GEORGE   You said 'why is' and stopped. Were you going to
                say why is my father now a Director of the East
                India Company? Because, if you were, I know the
                answer. Lord Liverpool spoke for him.

FRANCES   And who spoke for him to Lord Liverpool?

                (Pause. GEORGE has no answer and knows he can
                never find one, except in tears and hopeless rage
                both of which he forbears.)

GEORGE   But why does Uncle Horatio hate you so much?

FRANCES   I don't know, George. Knowing him, there must be a
                good reason. I wish I knew what it was.

                (She turns to go as the LIGHTS FADE and the sound
                of a naval band is heard, together with the noise and
                cheers of a crowd. The music and cheering will

continue into and through the beginning of the next
scene.)

ACT ONE

Scene Two

LORD BARHAM's office at the Admiralty is set on
the R. side of a stage. LORD BARHAM is seated at
his desk and a SERVANT is standing nearby.

BARHAM	(to SERVANT) You had better show Vice Admiral Lord Nelson in, if only to stop that damn cheering.
SERVANT	Very good, my Lord.
	(He goes out L. as NELSON pushes in.)
NELSON	Well, my Lord. Have you read Collingwood's despatch?
BARHAM	I have hardly had time to digest my breakfast, let alone Admiral Collingwood's despatch.
NELSON	(sits on chair L. of desk) The French and Spanish fleets are now combined and in Cadiz, from where they must soon come out - perhaps very soon - pray God not too soon - but they must come out, that is certain, for Cadiz cannot supply so vast an armada for long.
BARHAM	How did you learn this?
NELSON	My Lord, I learnt the capacities of Cadiz as a supply base at my mother's knee.
BARHAM	I meant how did you learn the contents of Admiral Collingwood's despatch? It was addressed to me personally, and was under strict confidential cover.
NELSON	My house lies on the Portsmouth Road. Captain Blackwood is an old friend and he naturally stopped for supper last evening.
BARHAM	I see.
NELSON	This is the despatch, isn't it? (Without

permission he picks it up and glances at it.)   God,
old Coll writes worse with his good hand than I do
with my bad.

BARHAM   You realise that not even Mr Pitt has read this
despatch yet?

NELSON   I earnestly hope that you have at least sent a fast
runner to Downing Street with its main contents, Lord
Barham, for what Mr Pitt must certainly do now –

BARHAM   Perhaps you would be kind enough to tell me what I
should do now? By the way, the name is pronounced
Barham. (Bare'm.)

NELSON   I am very sorry, my Lord. A junior Vice Admiral
should at least know how to pronounce the name of
his First Lord.

BARHAM   I see no reason, it's a very new title and a very new
appointment.

NELSON   By God, I like you. I was told I wouldn't but I do.

BARHAM   Thank you, Lord Nelson. What was it that I should
do now?

NELSON   (rising and moving around the room)   Reinforce
Collingwood at Cadiz at once with every fighting ship
you have at your command. Now that you have, by
the grace of God, run Villeneuve and his whole
combined fleets into this trap in the south of Spain.

BARHAM   I trust that the Almighty is as grateful for the
compliment as I am, Lord Nelson. Both of us, I
feel, might think it more proper to pay at least some
token of respect to the skill of our admirals and to
one admiral in particular.

NELSON   Myself? Oh no. I gambled wildly and recklessly on
where Villeneuve had gone and the gamble paid off.
But I take no pleasure in having risked so much for
such a stake.

BARHAM   Your reputation is indeed a great stake, my Lord.

NELSON   Oh God, did you think I meant that?

BARHAM   I am sorry, your country of course is a greater one.

NELSON   A greater one? I love my reputation, as you know,
                but how can you measure one man's reputation
                against the safety of England? You talk like an
                English Jacobin.

BARHAM   Our English Jacobins have grown something more
                patriotic. Their love of England keeps pace with
                their diminishing ardour to their infatuation of the
                Emperor Napoleon.

NELSON   I don't understand how a man's love of England can
                keep pace with anything except just England. You
                don't love England as you love a person or a thing or
                an idea. You don't even love it because it's your
                country. You love it because it's England, and if
                you don't love it you are damned. Voila tout, as the
                enemy might say. I don't doubt but that our English
                Jacobins would make mincemeat of that argument.

BARHAM   A statement of faith is hardly arguable, my Lord.

NELSON   I suppose not. Now will you do what I beg, and
                concentrate everything on Cadiz?

BARHAM   My Lord, I must have pause to consider –

NELSON   Why? Why pause for an instant? This chance may
                never come again. Oh, forget those invasion barges
                at Boulogne.

BARHAM   The presence of one hundred and fifty thousand
                enemy troops encamped twenty miles from Dover,
                who await only a fair wind and eight hours command
                of the channel to invade these shores is not, I think,
                a matter that should be forgotten by the occupant of
                this desk. Nor I think should it be forgotten that if
                these troops do land we have only pitchforks to fend
                them off.

NELSON   It should be forgotten now. More than that it must
                be.

BARHAM   But if we concentrate all our forces away from the
                channel –

NELSON   You will destroy all theirs.

BARHAM   But just supposing they destroy all ours? What
                then?

NELSON   I imagine you will have another Bonaparte brother
                as king at Windsor. But they won't destroy all ours.
                Did they at the Nile? Or at Copenhagen?

BARHAM   They were both brilliant victories, my Lord, but in
                neither battle did we commit our whole navy. If we
                had lost both battles we could still have survived.

NELSON   Is that what we are fighting this war for, Lord
                Barham, to survive?

BARHAM   No. But there are many who believe that just by
                holding out on this island and keeping our navy in
                being we may yet achieve peace.

NELSON   Peace with Napoleon? It is treason even to think it.
                Barham, this man means to master the world. He
                has openly proclaimed so many times. Now to
                master the world he must first destroy this island.
                This island must therefore destroy him. That is
                hardly arguable, is it?

BARHAM   As your Lordship puts it, no. But what might merit
                debate is exactly how this island is to manage the
                job.

NELSON   Not by skulking behind a ditch, waiting for him to
                cross it. By crossing it ourselves and attacking
                him. Not with pitchforks either, but with an
                expeditionary force armed with the best weapons our
                factories can make.

BARHAM   Where do we land it?

NELSON   Anywhere. Europe's coast line is three thousand
                miles long. Even Napoleon can't be everywhere at
                once. But I would advise Mr Pitt to look closely at
                the Kingdom of Naples, where our troops were
                recently engaged, and which has proved to be
                Napoleon's Achilles' heel.   (Carelessly.)   I
                don't say that on grounds of personal attachment,

just in case you think I do.

BARHAM   (carefully)   I had heard of your Lordship's strong
friendship for the exiled King and Queen of Naples.

NELSON   (having fun)   And not for the widow of our late
Ambassador there?

BARHAM   I read my newspapers.

NELSON   And perhaps find a moment to glance at the
cartoonists in St James's Street?

BARHAM   (stiffly)   Seldom, my Lord.

NELSON   You should more often. Some are very witty, I
assure you – although they are apt to portray Lady
Hamilton as somewhat too large and myself as
somewhat too small. But one doesn't expect to find
the exact truth in cartoons. Where were we?

BARHAM   Attacking Napoleon at Naples.

NELSON   Ah, but not only Naples. In Portugal and Spain, for
instance. Another expeditionary force landed, say
at Lisbon –

BARHAM   (abruptly)   Pardon my interruption, Lord Nelson,
but this is the Admiralty, and not the War Office.
How can we attack anywhere on the continent of
Europe without full and unchallenged command of
the seas?

NELSON   Well, of course, we must have that.

BARHAM   (barking)   How?

NELSON   But I have just been telling you. By annihilating the
enemy's fleet at Cadiz. If you reinforce Collingwood
with everything that you have, we may at last begin
to win this war.

BARHAM   May I be blunt? Does 'everything that I have' include
Nelson?

NELSON   No.   (Pause.)   I must remind your Lordship of
what I told you two days ago, when you awarded me
sick leave. I remain a very sick man.

BARHAM	Too sick to go out again, my Lord?
NELSON	Too sick to be capable of going out again, my Lord.
BARHAM	It will grieve Mr Pitt. He will certainly want it. So, of course, will the country.
NELSON	The country and Mr Pitt expect too much of me. (Angrily now.) Lord Barham, I am crippled, blind, infirm and nearly dead with service of Mr Pitt and my country. And I am not now needed. The ships and the men and the commander for the battle will be the best that we have, and when they come on the enemy the plan of battle is already laid out -
BARHAM	Your plan, my Lord?
NELSON	(shrugging) If Collingwood uses it it will be his. And he will use it, I'm sure. For complete annihilation it is the only one.
BARHAM	I would be interested to hear it.
NELSON	Perhaps another time. I am keeping a certain lady waiting. (He gets up.)
BARHAM	(rather stiffly) I am sorry, my Lord. Perhaps, at your convenience, you would draft it for me as a memorandum?
NELSON	I have already done so, my Lord. It will be delivered to you before the end of the morning.
BARHAM	I will be happy to study it, my Lord.
NELSON	May I take my leave?
BARHAM	Of course.

(NELSON suddenly changes his tone to one of desperate pleading.)

NELSON	Oh for the sake of Heaven, Barham, show some humanity! I haven't seen her for two years. Two years in a cabin, never a foot on shore, often ague-ridden, sometimes sea-sick, always racked with doubts and jealousies - (Hastily.) although no need, of course - by God there are many people I

might sue for slander if I had a mind – but the fevers
of the middle-aged lover know no reason – they
grow to an obsession –

(BARHAM is looking at his desk. It is hard for him
to look anywhere else.)

but enough of that. It was not what I meant to speak
of. You may regard it as a simple case – of a man
who hasn't seen his much-beloved mistress for two
years, and very little of her for five – for since I
was relieved of my command at Naples their Lord-
ships have been most diligent in keeping Lady
Hamilton and me apart. No, Barham, for the love
of Jesus, try to see my case!

BARHAM   I see your case, my Lord, and am indeed most
sorry for it.

NELSON   Then you will take that look of disapproval from your
face?

BARHAM   My face can hardly express what I do not feel. A
case such as yours is not one to be either approved
or disapproved. It is simply to be accepted.

NELSON   With understanding and compassion?

BARHAM   With compassion.

NELSON   I am rebuked.

NELSON   No, my Lord. I rebuke myself. I have too dull and
prosaic a soul to attempt understanding of such
gothic and extravagant matters as the fevers of a
middle-aged obsession.   (Proffering a document.)
Would you care to take this?

NELSON   What is it?

BARHAM   The Lords of the Admiralty's testimonial on your
recent operations in the Atlantic. It is quite worth
reading, and would only intrude an hour or two on
your Lordship's well-earned leisure.

(Pause. NELSON looks at BARHAM and still reads
that mark of official disapproval in BARHAM's face.

He takes the testimonial.)

NELSON   (bowing)   Your servant, Lord Barham - Barham.

BARHAM   (rising)   Lord Nelson.

(NELSON walks briskly out of the room, watched by
BARHAM. Again we hear the band, this time
playing a gay and popular theme of the time.

The LIGHTS FADE, and once more we hear the
distant sounds of cheering.)

ACT ONE

Scene Three

A light comes up on a painting of EMMA HAMILTON,
done in her extreme youth. Then, another light
shows us a very rumpled bed, with only its
occupant's hair showing. Finally all necessary lights
come on to show us the bedroom and boudoir of
EMMA HAMILTON in Clarges Street, London. A
screen in the bedroom area masks the powder room.

FRANCESCA, EMMA's personal maid, a middle-
aged Neapolitan of peasant extraction whom EMMA
has imported into England from Naples some years
before, but who has resolutely refused to learn more
than the barest minimum of English, is ushering
GEORGE MATCHAM into the boudoir. He looks
intensely nervous and is plainly determined to be on
his very best behaviour in such an exalted place.

FRANCESCA   (gesturing)   Io varo a eccellenza - ah non capista -
you wait - I go see.

(She goes into the bedroom area, leaving GEORGE
staring at the painting. FRANCESCA shakes her
Ladyship's shoulder.)

Eccellenza - eccellenza - eccellenza!

EMMA   (not stirring)   Fart off.

FRANCESCA   Eccellenza, il Signorino Matcham sta qua.

EMMA   (rolling over)   You're mad, Francesca. It's the middle of the night.

FRANCESCA   Vi piacerebbe, non è vero? Quante volte stanotte? 'Ow many times?   (She disappears behind the screen.)

EMMA   (calling after her)   Stai zitta, cretina.

(EMMA sits up. Her hair tousled from sleep and her eyes heavy from lack of it, she doesn't, naturally, look at her best. She blinks, yawns and stretches herself. FRANCESCA comes back with a tankard into which she is pouring porter. She hands it to EMMA.)

Con cognac?

FRANCESCA   Naturalmente.

EMMA   Not naturalmente at all. It just happens that this morning I happen to need it laced.   (She takes a swig and puts her other hand up to indicate the number seven.)

FRANCESCA   Eccellenza?

EMMA   I'm answering your question - seven times.

FRANCESCA   Seven? Ancora un anno a mare e - Pouff!   (She hands EMMA a mirror and a comb, and places a vanity box beside her.)

EMMA   You're an impertinent cow and I wonder why I keep you.

FRANCESCA   Pouff! Un no di vostra eccellenza e sarebbe la vittoria di Napoleone.

EMMA   (busy on her hair)   Me say no? It's not in my nature to say no, Francesca - not to anyone - but least of all to my Nelson. I don't much like what I see here. What's this young Matcham like?

FRANCESCA   Un ragazzo qualunque - normale - ordinario.

EMMA   No nephew of Nelson's can be an ordinary boy. How do I look?

FRANCESCA   Bellissima Emma Hamilton, come sempre.

EMMA   Bitch.   (Making a face at her.)   Bring him in.
                   And then get me another porter.

FRANCESCA   Con cognac?

EMMA   Pochissimo, pochissimo.

FRANCESCA   Mangiare dopo? Far este meglio.   (She takes the
                   tankard from bedside table and moves to bedroom
                   door.)

EMMA   My stomach wouldn't take food this morning.
                   (Shouting after her.)   Well - perhaps I'll toy with
                   a piece of cold mutton in my bath -

                   (FRANCESCA approaches GEORGE who is standing,
                   fidgeting with his hat.)

FRANCESCA   Sua eccellenza vi aspetta.

                   (GEORGE, not understanding, stands nervously.
                   FRANCESCA summons him with a gesture.)

                   Venite. Venite. Come. Come.

                   (GEORGE, frantically nervous, gives a last look at
                   the picture and then follows FRANCESCA into the
                   bedroom area, and up to the bed. As EMMA turns
                   her head to welcome him he stops uncertainly, plainly
                   wondering if there hasn't been some mistake.
                   FRANCESCA continues on into the powder room.)

EMMA   (holding out her arms)   My dearest little George
                   Matcham. Come here and let me kiss you.

                   (It is noticeable that whenever EMMA is not talking
                   to an intimate, as FRANCESCA plainly is, and is in
                   control of herself, as she is now, that she can
                   readily adopt a manner that does not confound belief
                   that she was once the British Ambassadress in
                   Naples. (Although even there a figure of fun to
                   visiting English gentry.) She has a fairly strong
                   accent (Lincolnshire, to be pedantically precise)
                   and a coarseness of expression that comes from an
                   honest refusal to pretend that her origins were

anything but the most humble and obscure; but with all that we can see the lady who has presided at Sir William's elegant and expansive dinner-tables, and who has been on terms of intimacy - extreme intimacy in many cases - with the greatest in the land.)

You must forgive me, little George, for receiving you in my bed, but this morning, for some reason, I am afflicted with the plaguiest migraine ever.

(FRANCESCA arrives with the tankard refilled and hands it to EMMA.)

(To GEORGE.)   Recommended by my doctor for just such occasions.

GEORGE   I'm so sorry, Lady Hamilton.

(FRANCESCA goes out R.)

EMMA   It will soon pass, I assure you.   (She toasts him and takes a gigantic swig, followed by an ill-suppressed belch. She squeezes his arm.)   Well, dear young George, aren't you excited to be here and coming down to Merton?   (She puts tankard on bedside table.)

GEORGE   Oh yes, of course I am.

EMMA   (looking at him)   Yes - I could have told you were a Matcham. Isn't it such splendid news, your father being made so important in the city?

(EMMA pats the bed and GEORGE sits. He nods unhappily.)

Oh, my Nelson had to work hard for him, I tell you. I kept him to it. We can't have any member of our family not looked up to. So you're young nephew George? The last of all the Nelsons to be welcomed to Clarges Street and Merton.   (Fondling him again and making him more nervous.)   Oh, we have had such a houseful at Merton this last week, all of the family, and such coming and going of Ministers and high ups, but them I don't give a fart

for, and that's the truth, George. It's my Nelson's
family only that I love - as I love everything that is
shared between me and him. His family is now
mine, George. You know that, don't you?   (She
begins to put on make-up from vanity box.)

GEORGE   Yes, my Lady.

EMMA   Don't call me my Lady.

GEORGE   What shall I call you?

EMMA   Aunt, of course, what else? Aunt Emma.
(Glancing at him.)   You favour your father, I see,
with perhaps a touch of my Nelson about the eyes -

GEORGE   (eagerly)   Oh, do you really think so?

EMMA   His poor eyes.   (Continuing to make herself up.)
Yes, you have, George. You're proud of that?

(GEORGE makes no answer to so obvious a question.
EMMA puts down make-up and picks up tankard.)

Of course you are. To be Jove's nephew gives you
a place on Olympus, too. I call him great Jove
sometimes to tease him, but it's not far from the
truth - my opinion.   (Flourishing her tankard.)
Great Jove, immortal of all immortals.   (She
nearly spills her porter.)   Oh, frig it! All over
the poxy bed -

(GEORGE rises and FRANCESCA comes in with
EMMA's dress.)

FRANCESCA   Quello di taffeta verde?

EMMA   Jesu Maria, no.

(FRANCESCA goes out with dress, then re-enters.)

There'll be a crowd outside. I don't want to look
like a curate's prick. I'd better come and choose.
Here -   (To GEORGE.)   hold this.   (She
hands him the tankard and climbs out of bed.)
Yes, George, your uncle is the perfect pattern of a
hero, to stand before this age and any other. A man
both great and good, and how rare that is in this

wicked world.

(She totters a little as FRANCESCA helps her into a peignoir taken from chair U.L. of bed.)

Hold me up, you silly cow.   (Seeing GEORGE's face.)   It's my migraine, George. And my Lord and I were a trifle late last night too -

GEORGE   At Court? I read there was a ball -

EMMA   (shortly)   No, not at Court. His Lordship and I - well, we don't frequent the Court. Not this one, anyway. Naples, of course, was different. The Queen of Naples - I count as perhaps my dearest friend in all the world. How I miss her.   (Sits on bed.)   You know, George, so close was Her dear Majesty of Naples and me that we would sometimes, when she was lonely or scared of those devilish Jacobins who murdered her poor sister, Marie - the martyred Antoinette - we would sometimes sleep all night together in the very same bed. And the King, he would do everything to honour me too, but not, of course, quite in the same way. But this old English absurdity and his German Frau, they're - well they're not really royal in my opinion.

(A FOOTMAN comes in with a card on a salver. He hands it to EMMA, who is engaged in swigging her porter. She reads it.)

Lord Minto - an old friend of my Nelson's, indeed of us both - but I haven't seen him for some time. (To FOOTMAN.)   Show him in here. He lives in Scotland - or somewhere. Quite in the wilderness - nowadays - although he was our Ambassador in Vienna, when me and my Nelson visited there - (To FRANCESCA.)   Will the water keep hot?

FRANCESCA   Ci stanno due brocche ancora piene.

EMMA   (to GEORGE)   He's coming down with us to Merton.

(MINTO comes in. He is middle-aged, very elegant in appearance and urbane in manner. GEORGE stands.)

MINTO	(bowing low over her hand) Dear Lady Hamilton, what an exquisite pleasure, after so long.
EMMA	I don't know that I'm speaking to you, Minto. Since Vienna you've avoided me like the pox.
MINTO	Dear Lady, since Vienna I've avoided everyone like the - plague who doesn't happen to live in Roxburghshire.
EMMA	That's not true, and I know it. You've been reported at Court many times.
MINTO	(shrugging) Ah. At Court. But nowhere else. (Sits on chair U.L. of bed.)
EMMA	You were at that ball last night, I'll wager.
MINTO	Oh yes. I looked for you and Lord Nelson.
EMMA	We weren't asked, and well you know it.
MINTO	An oversight, surely?
EMMA	Oversight, my arse. They won't have us, at any price. I don't mind for myself, but I do mind for him. Two years away, the West Indies saved and then - not so much as a coffee at the Palace. No more of that. I can only say, Minto, it doesn't take you long to leave your beloved Roxburghshire when you hear my Nelson's back in England. Not that I'm not glad to see you, of course.
MINTO	I had some business in town.
EMMA	You didn't have some business in town when it was to see me, did you? Only to see my Nelson. (To GEORGE.) Lord Minto is loved by Lord Nelson best of all persons in the world - second only to me, of course. Isn't that true, Minto?
MINTO	I would be happy to think so, my Lady. But you should have added that I run you a very poor second, for the competition provided by your Ladyship is, to say the very least, large.

EMMA   (covering up that part of her body to which his eyes
                have momentarily strayed)   Large?

MINTO   I meant that I unhappily possessed neither the
                figure nor the gender to compete in such a race –

EMMA   Every word you say makes it worse, you beast. Oh!
                This is young George Matcham, my Nelson's
                nephew.

MINTO   (stands and bows)   Master Matcham.

GEORGE   (bowing)   Lord Minto.

                (For the rest of the scene both EMMA and MINTO
                continue to ignore him. GEORGE sits unhappily on
                the bed where he has been pushed by EMMA, holding
                the tankard from which EMMA takes an occasional
                sip. FRANCESCA has gone back into the powder
                room.)

MINTO   (to EMMA)   I assure your Ladyship that my
                compliments to you, clumsy as they are, bear no
                allusion whatever to your most handsome embonpoint
                – which suits you, as always, quite admirably.

EMMA   If you did possess my gender, I'd just call you bitch
                and have done. Oh well, it's happiness makes me
                fat – and, let me tell you, Minto, I've heard no
                objections about that from the only source that
                matters.   (Rises and crosses to large mirror on
                dressing-table.)   Anyway, when my Nelson goes
                to sea again next year, I'll pine away to a shadow,
                see if I don't.

MINTO   Next year?

EMMA   (savagely)   Is he not due a year's rest?

MINTO   (shrugging)   He's due a lifetime.

EMMA   A lifetime wouldn't last him long if you and your
                politician friends had your way. But you won't have
                your way – none of you. He's given me his word on
                that – and that's not lightly given.

MINTO   I know it isn't.

EMMA   Nor lightly broken, neither.   (Wagging an
                  admonishing finger at MINTO.)   So I want no
                  meddling, Minto - from you or anyone else. See?

MINTO   Meddling?

                  (They are on opposite sides of the bed, talking over
                  GEORGE's head.)

EMMA   I know you. Like all his fine friends you want the
                  two of us separated - by a thousand leagues of sea if
                  you can. You can't bear the thought of what might
                  lose your party a few boroughs at the next election.
                  Nelson living with a woman not his wife? Oh no - we
                  can't have the electors hear such wicked, malicious,
                  scandalous things about the man whose reputation
                  keeps Mr Pitt in Downing Street.

MINTO   I might perhaps remind your Ladyship that I am a
                  Whig, and that the House of Lords has anyway no
                  need to woo electors. I personally am therefore
                  absolved from your Ladyship's suspicions.

EMMA   Oh no you're not. Whig and Tory, Commoner and
                  Peer, King and Queen, you're all alike. You need
                  your Nelson, and you need him pure. There's not
                  one of you doesn't want to split us, and wouldn't say
                  afterwards it was done for England, not for your-
                  selves. Perish the thought! Well, let me tell you,
                  Minto, what England wants. England wants a live
                  and happy Nelson, not a Nelson broken and sick,
                  and half dead with longing. And as for me you don't
                  care that -   (Flicking her fingers.)   any of you.
                  Nelson dead and I'm thrown on to the dust-heap. Do
                  you think I don't know that, Minto? So - on this visit
                  - no meddling, do you hear?

                  (Pause.)

MINTO   The epithet 'bitch' I could perhaps agree to be
                  saddled with, my Lady, saving my gender, but
                  'meddler' never. So, may it just be 'bitch'?

EMMA   (with a rough, sincere laugh)   I could like you,
                  Minto, if you'd ever let me.

FRANCESCA   (appearing)   Il bagno di vostra eccellenza si sta raffredando.

EMMA   Vengo. Vengo. Aspetto. Un momento. I got angry with what you said about 'large'. Yes, you caught me there, I'll grant. Still would you have me a flagpole?   (Laughing again.)   Perhaps you think my Nelson would, so that he could more easily run up his flag? But his flag does well enough as it is, thank you very much.

(She takes a large swig of her tankard, from GEORGE, while MINTO joins in her laughter.)

Last night it was nailed to the mast, at 'no surrender' and with the signals all at 'close action'.   (She laughs again, and handing the tankard back stops at the sight of GEORGE.)   George, into the next room with you.

GEORGE   (keen to go)   Yes, Lady Hamilton.

EMMA   Aunt Emma.

GEORGE   Sorry. Aunt Emma.

(GEORGE goes into the boudoir. EMMA stops MINTO from joining him.)

EMMA   Did he understand that?

MINTO   At that age they understand most things, and enjoy them just as keenly as your Ladyship.

(EMMA appears at the entrance to the boudoir. She sees GEORGE studying the painting again and moves towards him.)

EMMA   Not more interested in the dead painting than in the live model, George?

GEORGE   (turning to face EMMA)   Oh no, most assuredly not –

EMMA   Assuredly? If I could have spoken like that at his age I might have ended a duchess.

MINTO   (entering the boudoir)   You may yet end a duchess.

EMMA

Emma, Duchess of Bronte, Viscountess Nelson?
There's a certain much-to-be-hoped-for event that
has to take place first, might I remind you. But
they do say the winters at Bath aren't too healthy
for the rheumatical.

MINTO

They have indeed reported a certain malignancy of
vapours there.

EMMA

(raising her tankard)   Good luck to the vapours,
say I and don't let them spare any Toms, or any
Tits. By which I don't mean something vulgar,
Minto - like what you've been staring at this last
five minutes.   (Calling to GEORGE.)   George,
talk to Lord Minto now, but don't listen to a word he
says about me, because he hates me like the pox -
which is nothing, of course, save the greatest
jealousy.

MINTO

Who now, my Lady, is thé bitch?

(EMMA, on her way towards the powder room,
laughs, finishes her tankard and disappears behind
the screen. MINTO approaches GEORGE.)

Do I need to tell you that what our hostess just said
is a joke?

(GEORGE, discomfited and bewildered, is silent. It
seems safest. MINTO pours himself out some wine
from a tray of drinks on a table.)

Will you join me?

GEORGE

No, thank you.   (Sits L. of table.)

MINTO

Not allowed it?

GEORGE

Oh, I'm allowed it.

MINTO

Then have some.   (He pours a glass and hands it
to GEORGE.)   It might help to remove that look.

GEORGE

What look?

MINTO

To meet Lady Hamilton, for the first time, can, I
know, be rather a shock to a juvenile sensibility.

Never, I dare say, more than to a nephew of Lord Nelson's. Your look is one of surprise, Master Matcham. Remove it. It will not be popular at Merton. Your good health, sir.

GEORGE   (sipping)   My Lord.

MINTO   (appreciatively)   She keeps a good wine. I wonder who pays for it. Not your uncle, I trust. He has not prize money enough for even a pipe of this.

GEORGE   I thought Lady Hamilton was rich.

MINTO   Rich in everything but money. Sir William left her only his debts.

(GEORGE has turned to look at the portrait again. Pause. MINTO indicates the painting.)

As a Bacchante. She was then, I believe, sixteen. A rather mature sixteen, of course.

GEORGE   (turning slowly)   Are you fond of Lady Hamilton?

MINTO   You seem, Master Matcham, to have inherited your uncle's flair for surprise attacks.

GEORGE   I'm sorry.

MINTO   (crossing to above GEORGE)   Don't be. I am fond of Emma Hamilton. She's a very generous and good-hearted lady - loyal, passionate, and kind.

GEORGE   Kind?

MINTO   Very kind. Except, of course, to her enemies - but as they are mainly Neapolitan revolutionaries -

GEORGE   I was thinking of an enemy nearer home.

MINTO   (frowning)   Ah. But why fret about her either?

GEORGE   She's my aunt.

MINTO   An aunt, superseded by events. You now have an Aunt Emma. You had better have some more of this. You still have that look.   (Takes GEORGE's glass and crosses to table.)

GEORGE   (pointing to the picture)   If you could only explain -

MINTO   Explain what?

GEORGE   It doesn't matter. I shouldn't ask.

MINTO   (crossing to GEORGE with glass)   I don't think
                you should, Master Matcham.   (Raising his hand
                to stop GEORGE's apology.)   Not because the
                question is likely to be improper but because it is
                likely to be unanswerable.   (Turns chair L. of
                table to face GEORGE and sits.)   What does
                Lord Nelson see in her? Is that what you want
                explained?

                (GEORGE nods.)

                What does one person see in another person? That
                question has been asked since the beginning of time
                and will be asked to the end of it - and there is very
                rarely any answer, Master Matcham.

GEORGE   But he's a great man.   (Passionately.)   You do
                believe that, don't you?

MINTO   Oh yes.

GEORGE   Great because of what he has done or because of
                what he is?

MINTO   I think you should refer that question to Captain
                Hardy, his Flag Captain. He can speak for him in
                both capacities better than I. I can only speak for
                him as a man in love.

                (Pause.)

GEORGE   Above all things I don't understand how he could allow
                Lady Hamilton to treat his wife the way she does.

MINTO   Your ex-Aunt Frances? In what way does she treat
                her? Does she send poisoned pork pies to Bath?

GEORGE   (angrily)   She's bribed his whole family to desert
                her.

MINTO   (shrugging)   They've deserted her readily enough,
                and I'd say that any bribes have been his, not hers.

GEORGE   (stiff with rage)   Oh no! That's a lie.

              (Pause.)

MINTO   Master Matcham, you are not quite old enough yet to
              challenge and not quite young enough to put across
              my knee - I really think you must withdraw that
              observation.

GEORGE   I'm sorry - I'm very sorry, my Lord - but it
              couldn't be Lord Nelson. It just couldn't be - that's
              all I meant -

              (Pause. MINTO looks at him thoughtfully.)

MINTO   (shrugging)   Very likely not. It hardly matters,
              anyway, as the wife in question is, I hear, perfectly
              content with her two thousand a year, and her
              reflected glory in the society of Bath.

GEORGE   That is not true -

MINTO   (smiling)   Again, sir?

GEORGE   I mean I know that isn't true. I've seen her recently
              and she's very - well - upset.

MINTO   Really? Tears? You'll learn one day that the tears
              of a neglected but comfortably pensioned-off grass
              widow aren't always very real.

GEORGE   Hers were real.

MINTO   When did you last see her?

GEORGE   A week ago, and she gave me a letter to deliver to
              her husband.

              (Pause.)

MINTO   You must, of course, on no account, deliver it.

GEORGE   My Lord, I must.

MINTO   Must?

GEORGE   I gave my word.

MINTO   Oh God, deliver me from a schoolboy's honour!
              Do you want to destroy your uncle's peace of mind?

GEORGE   Oh no! Oh Heavens, no!

MINTO   Then give me that letter and let me tear it up. Or, better still, return it to her unread.

GEORGE   It's already been returned to her opened and unread. That's why I'm taking it down, so that this time he'll receive it at least.

                (Pause. MINTO has entirely lost his urbanity. Of the two he is now the one to seem shocked.)

MINTO   Who returned it?

GEORGE   Mr Davidson.

                (A pause. MINTO rises.)

MINTO   But Davidson doesn't take his orders from Lady Hamilton.

GEORGE   Still she must have opened it, and told him it was a bad, vile letter, full of abuse and that he mustn't read it. Then she must have got him to order Davidson to send it back. That's how I've worked it out.

MINTO   (thoughtfully)   I have no doubt at all that you are perfectly right, Master Matcham, and that above all else is why I want that letter kept from Lord Nelson, and I want you to give it to me now.

GEORGE   No.

MINTO   I am a pacific man and deplore violence, but it has occurred to me that on this occasion I might well be forced to use it.   (Menacingly.)   You will give me that letter at once, sir.

GEORGE   It's under lock and key.

MINTO   You have the key on you?

GEORGE   No.   (With bravado.)   You can put your sword to my throat, my Lord, but I'll give that letter to only one man; the man to whom it was addressed.

                (Pause.)

MINTO   You have been seeing Master Betty on the stage recently?

GEORGE   I saw him at Bath.

MINTO   I don't happen to be wearing a sword, nor indeed have I these twenty years. This is no matter for boyish heroics, sir. You have a charge of gunpowder under lock and key and you apparently intend to ignite it in your uncle's face.   (Crosses to sit R. of table.)   And all because a jealous wife squeezed out some easy tears into your lap.

GEORGE   (after a pause, quietly)   She cried the way I've never seen anyone cry before in my whole life. She cried from deep, deep down in herself, as if she were ill. I'll never forget it as long as I live.

MINTO   Then at least keep it to yourself.

GEORGE   Why should what's happened make him turn so much against his wife?

MINTO   I don't know, and nor does anyone else. But I must earnestly beg you not to deliver to him that letter.

(GEORGE shakes his head.)

(Urgently.)   You can at least postpone delivery a little.

GEORGE   I must give it to him before I leave Merton.

MINTO   Where is Lady Nelson? Still in Bath?

GEORGE   No, in London, at her house in Somerset Street.

MINTO   (rising and crossing to drinks)   Then I shall have to speak to her most urgently, which will put me in the unlikely role of trying to put out a fire in a powder magazine. I have no doubt but that I'll be blown to pieces, with no posthumous medal for gallantry to console my family.

(EMMA flies out of the powder room struggling into her peignoir, and runs across the bedroom into the boudoir.)

EMMA   He's brought the biggest crowd yet. I was looking
              out of the closet window.

              (GEORGE crosses to above C. table.)

MINTO   Was that quite wise, my Lady?

EMMA   Oh, you're such a prude. The crowd have often seen
              me with nothing on. They like it.

MINTO   I'm sure, but -

EMMA   (interrupting)   They were holding up babies for
              him to bless.   (Hugging GEORGE.)   Oh George,
              aren't you proud?

GEORGE   Yes.

EMMA   I nearly huzzaed myself out of the window.
              (Crosses to C.)

MINTO   That would have pleased the cartoonists -

EMMA   The cartoonists? Those buggers aren't worth my
              piss -

              (NELSON comes in L. He is dressed as when we
              last saw him, having come from the Admiralty. He
              looks only at her, ignoring MINTO and GEORGE.)

              You kept your promise?   (Crosses to NELSON.)

NELSON   Did you doubt me?   (He embraces her ardently.)

EMMA   In that poxy Admiralty I always doubt you. Those
              people in there could get you to go out tomorrow.
              Did you ask for a year?

NELSON   I didn't specify.

EMMA   (angrily)   You promised -

NELSON   I just told him I wasn't going out now, to Cadiz - and
              repeated that I was on sick leave. But it'll be a year,
              my heart, never fear. A whole year - I promise.

EMMA   (kissing him)   Oh I do fear, Nelson.

NELSON   Don't.   (He gives her a long, possessive embrace.)

EMMA	(breaking away) We have company.
	(NELSON sees the other two. Plainly he has difficulty with his eyesight.)
NELSON	Why, Minto.
MINTO	Lord Nelson. (MINTO crosses to NELSON.)
NELSON	You have obeyed your summons! By God, I'm most heartily flattered. (He embraces him.) And more happy to see you than I can properly tell you. You've grown thin. We'll alter that at Merton. Emma is the most perfect housekeeper in the world – if a thought extravagant in these days of high prices.
EMMA	Enough of that, Nelson. All's done for you and no one else. (Pointing to GEORGE.) This is Master –
NELSON	(crossing U.C. to GEORGE) I know who this is. Dear nephew George! My dearest, dearest boy! How good to see you! But you have grown so much I had pains to recognise you. By God, you look older than I did when I was first made a captain, doesn't he, Emma?
EMMA	How do I know? When you were first made a captain we hadn't met.
NELSON	(smiling at her) Perhaps that is just as well.
EMMA	Nelson!
NELSON	(hastily) For the Navy's sake, I mean, not my own.
EMMA	But that's worse. Do you want young George to think that his Aunt Emma's influence on Nelson has been bad for the country?
NELSON	(to GEORGE, quietly) All I meant, George, was that to have met Lady Hamilton as a youth might – to the detriment of my later service – have made me chary of risking a life suddenly grown too precious to lose.

EMMA   That's better. He can turn quite a phrase for a
                        sailor, can't he?

NELSON   (suddenly noticing)   Emma, why are you undressed
                        before these men?

EMMA   Oh, they're not really men, Nelson - I mean one's
                        a boy and the other's a - well, he's from Roxburgh.

                        (GEORGE sits on chair R. of C. table. A FOOTMAN
                        comes in with a card on silver salver. EMMA takes
                        it and reads it.)

                        Captain Hardy. Show him up.

                        (The FOOTMAN goes.)

                        Hardy, I'll agree, does count as a man. What's
                        more he thinks I'm the whore of Babylon even when
                        I'm in my winter woollies. I'll not be long.
                        (Moves towards bedroom.)

NELSON   (crossing to her)   May I come in with you?

EMMA   You'd best receive your precious Hardy here first,
                        hadn't you?

NELSON   I'm not anxious to. You of all people know why.

EMMA   Coward! Scared of his own Flag-Captain! What a
                        hero! You tell him now and get it over.

                        (She kisses him and then goes out into the bedroom,
                        where FRANCESCA is waiting, and they both
                        disappear behind the screen.)

NELSON   The crowd seemed even bigger than after Copenhagen.
                        It's surprising after two years. Oh, how I long
                        sometimes to walk in London unrecognised - but how
                        can I do it?

GEORGE   (taking it literally)   Perhaps, Uncle Horatio, if
                        you didn't wear all your stars and decorations -

NELSON   (after a faint pause, good-humouredly)   You're
                        quite right, George. It's my vanity that betrays me.

GEORGE   Oh, I didn't mean that.

NELSON   (to MINTO)   The boy's right, Minto. Even for an interview with the First Lord, I could wear a plain suit.   (Crosses to sit L. of table.)   I am on leave.   (Touching his four stars with a smile.) But damme, I like people to know what I've done! (To MINTO.)   I suppose, Minto, that you'd call that babyish?

MINTO   (crossing to NELSON)   Will you never forgive me for that unfortunate remark?

NELSON   No, by God, I won't.   (To GEORGE.)   He once told me that ashore I was a babe in arms, while at sea – well, no matter –

MINTO   At sea, an Alexander.

NELSON   Was it Alexander? Well, George, in both he exaggerated deeply –

FOOTMAN   (entering)   Captain Hardy.

(HARDY comes in L. He is a veteran sailor, at home in any company in the world, except, possibly, where he finds himself now.)

NELSON   Hardy.

HARDY   My Lord.

(NELSON rises and embraces HARDY without a word, and then turns to introduce GEORGE.)

NELSON   My nephew, George Matcham.

(GEORGE rises, bows, then sits. HARDY bows.)

And Lord Minto, whom I expect you know –

HARDY   (shaking hands)   Why yes. It's a great pleasure.

MINTO   Mine, too, Captain.

(There is an uneasy pause. NELSON is plainly nervous.)

HARDY   Her Ladyship?

NELSON   Is getting ready. I think perhaps – if you'll excuse

	me - (He goes towards the bedroom.)
HARDY	Before you go - you must tell me - is the rumour true?

(Pause. This is the moment NELSON has dreaded.)

NELSON	What rumour?
HARDY	That Villeneuve has trapped himself in Cadiz, with the whole enemy fleet?
NELSON	Yes, Hardy, it's true.
HARDY	(excitedly) I could hardly believe it, that after two years chasing we'd catch him at last, for he must come out of there soon, mustn't he?
NELSON	Yes, he must.
HARDY	How many ships?
NELSON	Something over thirty.
HARDY	And how many can we muster?
NELSON	Enough.
HARDY	As many as theirs?
NELSON	Who wants as many as theirs, Hardy? I said enough.

(HARDY laughs delightedly, and clutches NELSON's arm.)

HARDY	That's good. So when do we sail?

(Pause.)

NELSON	You will probably receive your orders to sail Victory south very soon for it's sure that Admiral Collingwood will need every ship that can be spared.

(Pause. NELSON plainly hates the look of growing disappointment he sees in HARDY's expression.)

HARDY	Admiral Collingwood?
NELSON	Yes. The Victory's still a good enough ship for the kind of pell-mell battle that Collingwood is likely to have to fight. Perhaps he will choose to fly his flag

in her rather than the Royal Sovereign. I know I
would, if I had my choice, in spite of the Royal
Sovereign's new copper and the Victory's barnacles
of two years -   (With a slightly embarrassed bow.)
Captain Hardy.

HARDY   (equally embarrassed)   Lord Nelson.

NELSON   It's good to have you with us, Minto.

               (NELSON goes into the bedroom and sits on the bed,
               staring at the floor, quite motionless.)

HARDY   I need some rum.

MINTO   I don't think she keeps it.

HARDY   (fiercely)   Not keep rum? What kind of an
               Admiral's lady is she -   (Crosses to drinks.)

MINTO   In some things - unsuitable.

HARDY   In some things?

MINTO   (crossing to C.)   There's good wine, Captain.
               And brandy, of course.

HARDY   French muck.   (Angrily.)   There's nothing
               here that's English at all. Yes, there is.   (He
               holds up a bottle.)   Gin. A whore's drink. Well,
               I'll have it. This is suitable, wouldn't you say, my
               Lord?

MINTO   (gently)   He has been away for two years, Captain.

HARDY   Yes. And so have I. Your health.   (To GEORGE.)
               Sir.

               (He pours himself some gin and downs the drink in
               one, replenishes, and then sits down L. of table in
               morose abstraction. MINTO glances from GEORGE
               to HARDY and then back again - two figures both
               showing clear traces of shock and disillusion.)

MINTO   (after a pause crosses to above table and, with a
               hint of mischief)   You may settle a point for our
               young friend, Captain. He asked me earlier if your
               Admiral is accounted a great man for what he has

done, or for what he is. I told him to refer that
question to you.

HARDY   (after a pause, gruffly)   He is great in both. How
could he have done what he's done without being
what he is?

MINTO   (to GEORGE)   You are well answered.

GEORGE   You mean he wouldn't have won his battles without
genius?

HARDY   Genius? Genius is nothing at sea. Nothing much,
anyway. It's keeping to windward of the enemy line
and attacking it at the right place and the right time
– that's part of his genius. I meant something much
more than that. I meant having the right ships and
the right men to attack with.

GEORGE   (puzzled)   Our ships and seamen are surely much
better than the French –

HARDY   That's what you read. Man to man and ship to ship,
I'm not so sure, myself. But if they are the best
who made 'em so?

(In the bedroom NELSON suddenly gets up from the
bed, his depression apparently over. He walks
behind the screen into the powder room.)

(Fiercely.)   Do you know the kind of man a
British seaman is, Master Matcham? 'Hearts of
oak are our men'? Don't you believe it! Pressed
into service as like as not – four-fifths of them are –
and pressed means kidnapped in Chatham or Portsmouth, knocked on the head and thrown into a life as
brutal and slavish as any in the world. In Newgate
gaol they get better to eat than maggoty biscuit, and
they don't get two hundred lashes of the cat o' nine
tails for a back answer to their gaoler.   (Rises to
above chair L. of table.)   Two hundred multiplied
by nine? That's a lot of bloody flesh off any man's
back, Master Matcham, and the threat of it keeps
'em servile enough – as it'd keep you too – and Lord
Minto, I don't doubt.

MINTO   Most certainly.   (Crosses to drinks.)

HARDY   And a bumper tot of rum would make you both drunk
             enough to fight a battle. But would you care over-
             much who won it? I ask you that straight, both of
             you? If you were British seamen would you break
             your hearts if the revolutionaries won their war
             against us or the tricolour flew in Parliament Square?
             And would you raise that bumper tot of rum to the
             health of your Admiral?

GEORGE   (quickly)   Before the battle of the Nile the men did
             drink to Nelson.

HARDY   Yes, sir. To Nelson. That's your answer.   (Sits
             L. of table.)   Those men do drink their rum to
             Nelson. They beg to serve in any squadron he
             commands and cry like women when they hear he's
             wounded. Don't ask me how he's done it, but if it's
             not by a miracle, and it isn't, then it must be by
             being the kind of man he is.   (Looking at his
             glass.)   Do you know I'm not sure even this gin
             isn't foreign –

MINTO   They do make a passable gin in Naples.   (Pours a
             drink.)

HARDY   I wish to Heaven he'd never seen that God-forsaken
             place.   (Morosely.)   And if you two gentlemen
             care to repeat that remark I'll bear the consequences
             like a man.

             (EMMA comes out of the powder room, followed by
             NELSON. She is dressed for the drive to Merton.
             She is walking to the boudoir, but NELSON pulls her
             back and embraces her.)

MINTO   They could be heavy.

HARDY   They couldn't be much heavier than now. Colling-
             wood's flag in the Victory? I'll shoot it down myself.

             (EMMA enters the boudoir with NELSON behind her.
             HARDY and GEORGE rise.)

EMMA   Captain Hardy, what honour you do me!

HARDY   (rising and crossing to her)   It is I who have the honour, your Ladyship.   (He bows.)

EMMA   The crowd is now quite immense.   (To HARDY.) Did they give you a cheer, Captain, when you came to the doorstep?

HARDY   I am hardly known to them, my Lady.

EMMA   (graciously)   You should be, and, one day, you will be, I'm sure.   (With a wide gesture.) One day everyone about my Nelson will be known. Minto, you are to come in the carriage with us. My Lord thinks it more proper -   (Moves to below C. table.)

NELSON   (mildly)   The word I used was seemly, Emma. Propriety was not in my thoughts.

EMMA   Nor ever will be, I trust.

(FRANCESCA hurries from the bedroom and hands EMMA a flask which she whisks into her reticule. MINTO notices it.)

It's a long journey, Minto, and you might be glad of it.   (Crosses to GEORGE.)   George, you and Captain Hardy are to follow in the second carriage. You may tell the good people out there, if they ask, who you are. They'll know, of course, where you're going.

NELSON   (looking at him)   By Heaven, George, you <u>have</u> grown! You must tell your mother to get you a new jacket. When Fanny bought the children's clothes -

EMMA   (warningly)   Nelson, are you going to say something in praise of Tom Tit?

NELSON   (lightly)   Nothing ever in praise of Tom Tit. It's hardly praise to say she had a gift for buying children's clothes -

EMMA   I'll buy George several new suits before he goes - at the best tailors. That's a promise.

NELSON   And most Emma-like in its extravagance.

(Kissing her.)   Perhaps just one new suit.

EMMA   And new boots to go with them.   (She sweeps out L.)

(NELSON moves D.L. with MINTO on his R.)

NELSON   (to MINTO)   I'm glad you're travelling with us. We have a little matter of business to discuss. The question of a loan to be raised at my bankers – (Mischievously.)   and in such matters I am, as you know, a very great baby indeed.

MINTO   I'll not deny it.

(They follow EMMA.)

And as regards babies, I haven't yet asked about Horatia –

(By now they are out of the room.)

NELSON   (off)   Oh, Minto, she is such an exquisite little creature now. I'm so proud of her. And so is Emma –

MINTO   (off)   She would be five, or thereabouts –

NELSON   (off)   Four and five months exactly.

GEORGE   (to HARDY)   Can't we go down?

HARDY   No. Let them get their huzzas! We'll be anonymous, and follow later.

GEORGE   I'll go and watch at the door.

(He goes out L. HARDY, left alone, stares broodingly into his glass, and then up at the portrait of EMMA. Suddenly, with a violent gesture, he hurls the contents of his glass at it. He is pouring himself another gin when GEORGE returns, looking bewildered.)

HARDY   So. They are cheering heartily?

GEORGE   Some of them laughed.

HARDY   Did they?

GEORGE   (utterly appalled)   They laughed at <u>Nelson</u>!

(HARDY gulps his drink down and gives GEORGE a
friendly pat.)

HARDY   With Lady Hamilton. After you, sir, we are part of
             this cavalcade.

             (The LIGHTS FADE. The cheers, which have started
             a little earlier, grow to a crescendo and we hear the
             sound of a string orchestra playing some genteel
             melody that is no doubt a great favourite at the Pump
             Room at Bath.)

             ACT ONE

             Scene Four

             The hall of LADY NELSON's London home, set on L.
             side of stage. On the wall is a portrait of NELSON.
             LORD MINTO is on stage. LADY NELSON enters L.

FRANCES   What a pleasure, Lord Minto, and how very
             unexpected. I thought you were one of my husband's
             privileged guests at Merton. Or so it says in the
             'Times'.

MINTO   (kissing her hand)   Yes, but I shall be returning
             for dinner.

FRANCES   That doesn't give you very long then.   (She sits L.
             and indicates he is to sit R.C.)

MINTO   Most unhappily, no, and I am especially commanded
             not to be late.

FRANCES   Lady Hamilton is to give one of her exhibitions?

MINTO   She prefers to call them attitudes.

FRANCES   How amusing. They are rather more than attitudes
             I understand.

MINTO   Indeed - they would hardly be out of place on the
             stage at Drury Lane - except that they would be.
             Lady Nelson, you may be wondering why I am
             calling on you.

FRANCES   You wrote the word 'urgent' on your card, and so I
            don't wonder. I think I know. But I do wonder at
            your courage in coming here by daylight.

MINTO   Why?

FRANCES   This house, it is very carefully watched. Most
            visits are reported.

MINTO   Surely you exaggerate.

FRANCES   I exaggerate nothing. If I am spied upon in Bath, as
            I am continually, why should I not be spied upon here,
            in London? Believe me, Lord Minto, I am very
            grateful to her for the attention. When she ceases to
            bother about me I shall know that I have lost utterly.
            What was it you had to say to me?

MINTO   Rather to ask something of you.

FRANCES   Young George has taken you into his confidence?

MINTO   Yes.

FRANCES   That is what I had guessed.   (After a pause.)
            No, Lord Minto - I will not empower you to release
            my nephew from his promise. That is what you were
            going to ask, I assume?

MINTO   My Lady - a letter of such ancient date, and one that
            has already been returned to you -

FRANCES   It was not returned to me by my husband to whom it
            was addressed, but by his mistress. But if my
            nephew George cares to break his promise that is his
            affair. You may tell him from me that I won't be
            angry.

MINTO   If I tell him that it will bind him even more strongly to
            his word of honour.

FRANCES   Yes, he is an honourable boy, my nephew George.

MINTO   You realise that your honourable nephew may well be
            blamed for his part in this affair?

FRANCES   But why? He has an honourable uncle.

MINTO   My Lady, forgive me, but in breaking an agreement of silence between you and your husband, are you sure you are acting so honourably yourself?

FRANCES   There was no agreement of silence. There never has been.

MINTO   But there must then, have been some agreement between you to separate utterly?

FRANCES   No. None. You see, Lord Minto, it was not he who deserted me, but I who deserted him. He never wanted it so. I was needed. I was needed for respectability. When I failed him - and I did fail him, I suppose, he turned to his family - and for the same reason.

MINTO   With certain inducements -

FRANCES   Large ones. I don't blame them.

MINTO   My Lady, what do you hope to gain by this?

FRANCES   The truth.

MINTO   The truth is that this is the woman he has chosen, the woman he now loves and who loves him - the woman he will never leave - ever, my Lady - from now till doomsday. Do you understand that?

FRANCES   No man could love that woman for life. That is not possible, my Lord. She knows it well and she is already afraid.

MINTO   Doomsday will not happen very soon.

FRANCES   No, but it will happen.

MINTO   Is it worth your waiting?

FRANCES   Yes.

MINTO   For how long?

FRANCES   For ever.

MINTO   Do you speak of eternity, Lady Nelson?

FRANCES   No, Lord Minto, I speak of his old age. That at least

will be mine. As was his youth. (Rising.)
Well, my Lord, I must not keep you any longer.

(MINTO rises.)

I would see you to the door, but I do not walk so well
these days - rather bird-like as you may have heard.
Lord Minto.

(He kisses her hand.)

You may tell young George that if he has any doubt
at all about the contents of that letter, he has my full
permission to read it and to judge of its propriety
himself.

MINTO
I shall do so. But I am not a very brave man and
I'm afraid I can already hear the thunder of an
approaching battle royal.

LADY NELSON
Oh dear. I am indeed sorry to be the cause of such
melodramatics in your quiet little family circle.

MINTO
I must confess, Lady Nelson, that although on
certain matters we do not see eye to eye, I do most
truly admire your spirit.

LADY NELSON
Thank you. I have some need of it these days.

MINTO
I don't doubt it - but I earnestly advise you, Lady
Nelson, do not abuse that spirit with too much hope.
(Crosses R.)

FRANCES
(suddenly, fiercely) Lord Minto. If I am to give
up hope so then must they. They must cease to
picture me as the 'Invalid of Bath'. I am not in a
decline. I am not going to die. I will do anything for
my husband's happiness except to die. That, if you
care to, you may tell him - and as coming from me.
(MINTO says nothing, as she struggles with tears
that are plainly not so far distant, but succeeds with
a visible effort in overcoming them. Then, with the
aid of her stick, she manages a very passable
curtsey.) Lord Minto. (She rises again, her
back straight and her head held high.)

MINTO
(bowing) Lady Nelson.

(He goes. FRANCES stands motionless, her back
to the portrait of the young NELSON. As the
lights fade on the scene the portrait still glows
brightly – until that too fades into darkness.)

END OF ACT ONE

ACT TWO

The lights come on to show the central acting area which will represent
the drawing-room and the dining-room at Merton (M). Beyond the
dining-room area there lies a stair-case leading to the bedrooms.

At the moment it is the drawing-room - the larger of the two areas - on
which we will be concentrating, for EMMA is in the midst of an Attitude
and the lighting, at the beginning of the scene, will be almost entirely on
her, as she stands, clothed in classical costume, right arm upraised
and expression borrowed, probably, from Mrs Siddons. Behind her
there is a chaise longue.

EMMA	And so the great hero fell and all the nation mourned him! (Towards NELSON.) But of all who mourned him, none mourned him more piteously than the woman who had borne his child, the woman whom he had chosen of all women to love and to keep (She kneels.) and the woman who had cherished him in her bosom and loved him more than very life - Andromache of Troy!
	(By now we can see her audience. It consists of the GEORGE MATCHAMS, Senior and Junior, KATHERINE MATCHAM, the REV WILLIAM NELSON (elder brother by a year to NELSON), his wife, SARAH, his son HORATIO (GEORGE's age), MINTO, HARDY and another Captain - BLACKWOOD, who brought the Cadiz despatches. NELSON sits rather apart from the others, on a large armchair D.L. Much of EMMA's performance is inevitably directed at him. MATCHAM, MINTO and HARDY are standing behind SARAH and the REVEREND WILLIAM who are seated on two chairs L. BLACKWOOD is standing behind harpsichord stool with GEORGE and HORATIO to the R. of him. Two SERVANTS stand behind them. FRANCESCA acts as a kind of stage-manageress. KATHERINE MATCHAM provides background on a harpsichord, and is not as sure of her cues as is FRANCESCA, or as EMMA would like. EMMA crosses to above chaise longue.)

But she knew not yet what had befallen her great
husband -   (Hides her face.)

HARDY   (murmuring to MINTO)   Who <u>was</u> her great husband?

EMMA   (before MINTO can reply, transfixing HARDY with a
furious glance)   only that Hector had gone forth to
battle   (FRANCESCA takes stole from harpsichord.)
- Hector, son of the King of Troy -   (This, though
indisputably accurate, is an improvisation for HARDY,
who nods, satisfied.)   and Andromache sat in her
dwelling wearing a purple mantle trimmed with gold.

(She sits on chaise longue. This is FRANCESCA's
cue to drape EMMA's shoulders with a purple mantle,
and for EMMA to recline in a graceful mime of happy
expectation.)

And she bade her maidens make ready a bath for her
husband when he returned from battle.

(FRANCESCA curtseys and turns U.C. KATHERINE's
trilling music, indicative of maidens preparing a
bath, is interrupted by her nervous difficulty in
turning over a page, and she gets a very sharp glance
from EMMA.)

But suddenly a great cry goes up from the walls of
Troy and Andromache bounds from her couch -

(EMMA manages the bounding from the chaise longue
with a little deft assistance from FRANCESCA who
then sits on the end of the chaise longue while EMMA
crosses D.C. , dropping stole.)

FRANCESCA   Attenzione.

EMMA   - and runs towards the ramparts. What does she see?
(EMMA backs to chaise longue, turns to FRANCESCA
and kneels.)   Oh, most heavy sight! Not Hector
slain!   (To FRANCESCA.)   Oh say he is not
dead! Not dead? Not dead?

FRANCESCA   (firmly)   E morto.   (She adjusts the purple
mantle more becomingly on her mistress's shoulders.)

EMMA   Ah, say not so! Is my life, my love, my all, now
                only dust?

FRANCESCA   E polvere.   (She joins the audience, her duties
                now performed.)

EMMA   (rising, holding the ends of her stole)   Ah! Aah!
                Aaah!   (Three long cries of tragic grief. She
                crosses D.R.)   Has Hector gone and am I now
                alone?   (She speaks this quietly and with feeling.
                For one brief moment we might feel that she could
                have had some talent as a professional actress.
                But, in an instant, she has thrown her arms to
                Heaven and is well back into the 'heroic' style.)
                Then death, takest thou me too!   (She runs round
                to above chaise longue and catches KATHERINE
                with her stole.)   Ah, my maidens - come quickly
                all my maidens, and prepare my funeral pyre! For
                I must die with him -   (There is a certain amount
                of gesturing to imaginary maidens after which
                EMMA, unaided this time, lies on the chaise longue
                in an attitude of tragic despair, carefully once more
                arranging her mantle to fall in the correctly
                classical folds.)

MINTO   (meanwhile, whispering to MATCHAM SR.)   Did
                Andromache kill herself?

MATCHAM   (whispering back)   In Emma's version, anyway -

EMMA   (still arranging her folds)   Ah most lugubrious
                and heavy woe! Ah, day of misery! Ah, noxious
                and lamentable fate!

MINTO   (whispering to NELSON)   Who wrote the words?

NELSON   (indicating the REVEREND WILLIAM)   My
                brother William -

EMMA   Ah my maidens, my maidens! Most wretched of
                all mortals am I now!

                (The REVEREND WILLIAM had heard NELSON
                and is inclining his head to what he assumes is
                MINTO's approbation of his literary skills.)

The crown o' the earth doth melt, and withered is
the garland of the war! The odds is gone, and there
is nothing left remarkable beneath the visiting moon.

(FRANCESCA crosses to table above harpsichord to
get dagger.)

MINTO   (to NELSON)   Brother William?

(He has spoken a shade too loudly. EMMA gives him
a glare, and Brother WILLIAM is distinctly put out.
NELSON smiles, a shade nervously.)

NELSON   Sometimes a little of another   William –

EMMA   (loudly)   The soldier's pole is fall'n. Young girls
and boys are level now with men. Great Hector's
gone, and the mind boggles with simple disbelief.
(Reclines.)   The great defender of our native
home is slain, and all the nation bewail him –

(KATHERINE has slipped into the Dead March from
Saul.)

Husband, I come!   (EMMA clicks her fingers and
FRANCESCA brings her the dagger.)   Now to
that name my courage prove my title! I am fire and
air! I come, I come. Poor, poor Andromache!
Husband – ah, my husband!   (She stabs herself
and falls back on the chaise longue.)

(The REVEREND WILLIAM and BLACKWOOD start
to applaud.)

The rest is silence.

(She dies. There is loud applause. It must here be
noted that eye-witness reports of EMMA HAMIL-
TON's Attitudes almost unanimously ascribe to her
a singular talent for heroic acting, a pleasing
soprano voice and a marked predilection for going
a mile too far. All these qualities will have been
noticeable in the performance she has just given,
and any slurring of speech or unhappy impromptus
– the excerpts from 'Antony and Cleopatra' were not
in Brother WILLIAM's script – could on this

occasion be well excused by the fact that it is quite
late in the evening and that she has had a fairly full
complement of brandy and champagne. It is
noticeable that, after taking a gracious bow and,
while still curtseying to NELSON, she takes the
tankard that FRANCESCA has just filled for her from
bottles on table U. L., and sips it thirstily; and if we
are observant we will notice that what she is sipping
is indeed champagne liberally spiked with brandy.
NELSON crosses to EMMA, sits her on chaise longue
and stands R. of her.)

NELSON	Bravo, Emma! Bravo! (He kisses her.) You were never better, on my life.
MINTO	(crossing to chaise longue and sitting) Magnificent as always, dearest lady. It is not a piece I had heard from you before.
	(KATHERINE has risen from the harpsichord. She and the others talk among themselves.)
EMMA	It's a favourite. Tonight I was as nervous as a pregnant nun - saving your cloth, Reverend.
	(The REVEREND, who has moved to L. of chaise longue, saves his cloth with a smirk.)
MINTO	The very bravura of the performance makes that hard to believe.
	(GEORGE crosses to HARDY and HORATIO crosses to SARAH. The two SERVANTS serve drinks and straighten up the room.)
REV WILLIAM	You were splendidly lifelike. (To MINTO.) Those words from the other William were not my doing, my Lord. Lady Hamilton is sometimes pleased to make certain additions -
EMMA	Emma, brother! What's this 'Lady Hamilton'? Shall I call you 'Dean Nelson'? (Takes drink from passing FOOTMAN and pours it into her tankard, replaces glass.)
REV WILLIAM	(the most sycophantic of an unhappily sycophantic

family)   Oh, Heaven forbid!   (To MINTO.)
Dearest Emma, I was saying, is sometimes
inclined to insert certain passages of her own finding,
and Shakespeare's Cleopatra, it seems, is one of her
favourite heroines.

MINTO

Of course.

EMMA

What do you mean by that, Minto?

(REVEREND WILLIAM joins HARDY by harpsichord.
SARAH crosses to him and sits on stool.)

MINTO

Of course Emma Hamilton would have as her
favourite that other 'lass unparallel'd'.

EMMA

Lass unparallel'd? Well, I'll accept 'unparallel'd'
at any hour and at ten in the evening I'll even
believe in 'lass'.

(NELSON crosses to L. of chaise longue.
BLACKWOOD joins him. MINTO and EMMA are
alone.)

(Admiringly.)   You think quick, Minto. If you'd
said something about 'this dotage of our Admiral'
you'd have had this in your face.   (Turning to
BLACKWOOD.)   Captain Blackwood, you are new
to this house, and so new to my little entertainments –

(MINTO rises. GEORGE and HARDY move U.C.)

BLACKWOOD

(who has a stammer, increased by his present
nervousness)   At N-Naples once I had the
p-p-privilege –

EMMA

Of course, at Naples. Your frigate was in the Bay
and Sir William and I came aboard. What
programme did I give on that occasion?

BLACKWOOD

(miserably trying to remember)   It was – oh
dear – something cl-classical.

EMMA

Of course. But what?

BLACKWOOD

Oh dear. It was something – r-rather happier than
the performance you have just given, I meant
j-j-jollier –

(His nervousness is increased by NELSON's genial presence at his elbow.)

I mean it wasn't a l-lady m-mourning for her l-lover's death or anything l-like that -

EMMA   (unhelpfully)   Husband's death -

BLACKWOOD   Oh, husband's death. Yes. In Naples you gave us a j-j-jolly lady -

EMMA   My thoughts in Naples were perhaps something jollier, Captain. You don't remember the lady's name?

BLACKWOOD   (excitedly)   She was a B-B-Bacchante - that's what she was - of course - and you made her most abandoned and true to life.

EMMA   But my performance this evening - less jolly, I agree, how did you find that?

BLACKWOOD   Oh quite pitiful.   (Unhappily this is about the one word that has come out straight and clear. BLACKWOOD is instantly confused.)   I mean -

NELSON   (stepping in to the rescue)   The word you used to me about the performance, Blackwood, was affecting.

BLACKWOOD   Oh yes. Aff-affecting was what I meant. I was most deeply aff-aff-affected by the whole thing.

                (MATCHAM crosses with HORATIO to steps U.C. HARDY joins them.)

EMMA   I am flattered. It takes much, I am sure, to affect the gallant captain of the 'Euryalus'.   (To NELSON, hand over mouth.)   Oh! Have I made one?

                (MINTO crosses to MATCHAM.)

NELSON   No, my love. The name was most nobly remembered. It is in fact, Blackwood's 'Euryalus' that lately brought us the news from Cadiz about Villeneuve.

EMMA   Oh, of course. And he goes back in her tomorrow,
                   you said?

                   (She takes another glass of champagne and brandy
                   from FRANCESCA, whose continued presence in the
                   room - the other servants having left - seems
                   designed solely for this purpose. The NELSON
                   family is grouped together round the harpsichord,
                   and near door leading to stairs U. C. , standing
                   rather formally, their faces smirking obsequiously,
                   as if in the presence of Royalty. HARDY, the only
                   one of the important guests not to have congratulated
                   EMMA, wanders from the room, and we see him
                   walking through the hall area at the back towards the
                   dining-room, which eventually he enters. A map has
                   been laid out on the table and it would appear that
                   NELSON had been giving his captains a rough brief-
                   ing of the battle to come. HARDY studies the map
                   and begins to move some objects on the dining table.
                   EMMA has been most conscious of his exit from the
                   sitting-room.)

                   (To BLACKWOOD.)   You see, dear Captain, how
                   well rehearsed I am in all matters concerning
                   Nelson's fleet.

NELSON   (smiling)   Collingwood's fleet.

EMMA   Well, it would be my Nelson's if he were there.

BLACKWOOD   No doubt of that, my Lady.

NELSON   But he is not there. He is here -   (Sits on chaise
                   longue.)

EMMA   (sharply)   - and most happily here -

NELSON   Indeed outrageously happily here - so it remains
                   Collingwood's fleet, and it's Collingwood's fleet he
                   sets sail to rejoin tomorrow.

EMMA   (raising her tankard)   I wish you a fair wind,
                   Captain.

                   (BLACKWOOD bows and crosses to KATHERINE. To
                   NELSON.)

I suppose when Collingwood fights your battle they'll make him an Earl.

NELSON   Do you grudge him that?

EMMA   I wouldn't grudge Old Coll being made Arse-licker in Ordinary to His Majesty - so I could keep my Nelson here with me.   (Her arm is lovingly around him, and from a glance around, she evidently wishes HARDY were there.)   What was it - in my Andromache - affected you most, Captain Blackwood?

(HARDY appears in doorway of drawing-room and talks to MATCHAM. FRANCESCA, at a gesture, refills EMMA's tankard.)

BLACKWOOD   (who had hoped himself out of gunshot)   Ah. That is a qu-question. Well, Lady Hamilton, when you spoke of H-Hector, I was made to think of another even greater d-defender of his country -

(KATHERINE crosses to L. chair and sits. HARDY joins her.)

EMMA   Not too much so, I hope. This defender is alive and so I mean to keep him - despite the underhand work of some who call him their friend. But still Europe's great defender! Let me see, let me see. How does it go? Yes. His legs bestrid - but why past tense? - His legs bestride the ocean - in whose livery walks crown and crownets - realms and islands are as plates dropped from his pocket -

(SARAH crosses to MATCHAM and HORATIO on stairs.)

NELSON   Emma, dearest -

EMMA   I was quoting a speech of Cleopatra's.   (At HARDY.)   Moll-Cleopatra - as some officers in your fleet call me, I hear.

(MINTO crosses to HARDY's L.)

NELSON   (following her glance)   A very pitiful joke, my love.

(BLACKWOOD crosses to U.R. of harpsichord.)

EMMA

But those words are Shakespeare's - and they're as true of you as they were of that silly old antique Roman when spoken by his strumpet gypsy. Captain - are you listening?

(MINTO moves to behind D.L. chair.)

HARDY

(turning to EMMA)   No, my Lady.

(HARDY shakes his head politely. NELSON realising from experience all the signs of an incipient scene, speaks quickly and lightly.)

NELSON

In that scene her Ladyship of Egypt was something exaggerating, I think.

EMMA

(crossing to L. of chaise longue, loudly)   This Ladyship of England exaggerates nothing. When I see my pillar of the world I see great Jove himself -

HARDY

(to MINTO, quite audibly)   It's a wonder she can see anything at all.

(EMMA wheels on him, evidently meaning to let go with some of the 'gutter language' for which she is famed. But, more dangerously, if less uncomfortably, for all, she decides to speak quietly.)

EMMA

I heard that, Captain Hardy. This is my house, and if I should choose to toast the guest who does such honour to this roof in what to your puritan mind might seem a glass too many of brandy and champagne, that I think should be my affair and not yours, don't you?

HARDY

I do, my Lady, indeed. It was only that my puritan mind hadn't perhaps quite grasped the fact that this was your Ladyship's house.

(HARDY seems happy to answer a broadside with a broadside. NELSON quickly interposes himself to stop what could be, for him, the most disastrous battle of all.)

NELSON

(crossing to above chaise longue)   Merton is our

	house, Hardy - your house, everyone's house who comes to visit it. And most certainly it is Emma's. Emma, my dearest, Captain Hardy is anxious -
EMMA	(interrupting) You haven't yet spoken of my performance, Captain. I am afraid you were most heartily bored by my drunken posturings.

(SARAH and HORATIO exit upstairs.)

NELSON	Emma -
HARDY	Not bored, Lady Hamilton.
NELSON	(now severe) Emma, I must beg you to stop this stupidity. All that Hardy meant was -

(He sees rightly that EMMA is on the verge of losing all control, and he is still trying to smile.)

EMMA	(pushing NELSON aside) I know well all that Captain Hardy meant, and so does he. He meant that I'm not your wife, Nelson - not by virtue of Mother Church. Well, Captain - a pox on Mother Church! I am, by everything that is just and honest in this world, the true and only wife of this man here - the father of my child, Horatia -
NELSON	(warningly) Emma, please stop this now -
EMMA	(too far gone in her tantrum to stop anything now) To all people in this house, Captain - to my Lord's family, to my Lord's friends, to my Lord's servants even - I am Lord Nelson's wife. To the whole of England I am his wife - and a pox on that old madman of Windsor and his German bitch of a Queen!

(Family, BLACKWOOD and MINTO go out L.)

(Lying on chaise longue.)   There's my loyal toast, Captain Hardy! To the whole of the rest of England, I, Emma Hamilton, am the true wife of Lord Nelson.

HARDY	Excepting, I would suppose, to Lady Nelson.

(Pause, broken before EMMA can break it more

violently, by NELSON.)

NELSON   Hardy, that was unforgivable.

HARDY   I shall leave.

NELSON   No.   (As HARDY still moves away we hear the sudden rasp of authority in NELSON's voice.) You will stay here, Hardy. I command it - Hardy -

(HARDY stops. That is a voice he can never disobey. But EMMA is continuing.)

EMMA   Tell the bugger to get out of this house now, and never come back. Nelson, I command you -

NELSON   (turning to EMMA)   You command me in most things, Emma, but not in that.

EMMA   Oh, indeed? Then perhaps I should leave your Lordship's house. Francesca   (Crosses to below harpsichord.)   - have my carriage brought round at once -

FRANCESCA   Subito, eccellenza, subito.

NELSON   Francesca, you will pay no attention to that, and you will leave this room at once.

(FRANCESCA, frightened too by the sound of NELSON's seldom heard voice of command, bobs, and looks uncertainly at her mistress. Pause.)

FRANCESCA   (finally with a deep curtsey to the conqueror of Naples)   A vostro ordine, signore.   (Crossing herself as she hurries out upstairs.)   Jesu! Jesu!

NELSON   (turning to EMMA)   Emma, you will apologise to Captain Hardy for what you have just said about the King and Queen. Also to Captain Blackwood.

EMMA   Apologise? Are you mad?

NELSON   They are serving Naval Officers of his Majesty the King who must not ever be spoken of in such terms in their hearing. Never. Understand me?

EMMA   Because they've sworn a vow of loyalty to his old lunacy?

NELSON   Yes.

EMMA   And vows are such sacred things, aren't they?

NELSON   Yes.

EMMA   More sacred, I don't doubt, than vows sworn by certain persons in the bed-chamber.

NELSON   (quietly)   All vows are equally sacred, Emma. Some that are made unwillingly in church may have to be broken, but there's no happiness in that –

EMMA   Oh – no happiness. That's good. So that's where we are now, is it? More happily in Tom Tit's bed-chamber than in mine? Why don't you go back to it then, if that's how you feel?   (Crosses to D.R. of harpsichord.)

NELSON   (not raising his voice)   Emma, you are making yourself a spectacle to strangers – and above all things else in the world I hate that. If you will apologise to the Captain, we will forget it all.

EMMA   (scornfully)   And you'll love me after? You'll vow that?

NELSON   I will love you always. That needs no now. You know it.

EMMA   I don't know it. If I did there might be no need for apologies now.

NELSON   (sharply)   Do it, please, Emma – for my sake.

(There is a pause. EMMA finishes her drink.)

EMMA   I'll do better than you ask. To show them I meant no real disrespect, I'll sing them the National Anthem. Can I do fairer than that?   (Going to the harpsichord.)   And isn't it the proper way to round off a performance? Kitty? Where's Kitty?

(KATHERINE flies in breathlessly.)

KATHERINE   Yes, Emma dear?

EMMA   Kitty, I want you to play the National Anthem, while
I sing it.

(MATCHAM enters from L. to above harpsichord.)

KATHERINE   Oh, most gladly.

(She sits at the harpsichord and strikes up. The
rest of the family, evidently believing that the storm
is over, come back. EMMA waits for them before
beginning to sing. Then she turns to NELSON and
sings straight to him.)

EMMA   (singing)
Join we great Nelson's name,
First on the rolls of Fame,
Him let us sing.
Spread we his fame around,
Honour of British ground,
Who made Nile's shores resound
God save my King.

(And with a deep curtsey she makes perfectly plain
exactly whom she means as 'her King'.)

(Abruptly.)   That is the only verse I know - or
care to learn.   (Lies on chaise longue.)

(All look at NELSON to see how they should take
EMMA's 'apology'. He applauds politely.)

NELSON   I am, as always, most deeply flattered by those words,
Emma.   (Turning from her abruptly.)   Hardy,
shall we talk in the dining-room? Blackwood, will
you join us? You carry that despatch for details?

(HARDY and BLACKWOOD cross below harpsichord
towards dining-room.)

BLACKWOOD   Ay, ay, my Lord.

NELSON   If the rest of you should happen to be going to your
beds -

(It is a royal command and there is a general hasty
murmur of assent.)

then I'll bid you all a collective good night, and a most pleasant rest until tomorrow.

CHORUS OF
VOICES   Good night, brother, brother-in-law, uncle, etc.

(NELSON bows, and then quietly ushers HARDY and BLACKWOOD out of the room. We see the three men making their way to the dining-room. EMMA, now at the harpsichord, strumming some notes gently, laughs.)

EMMA   (to the departing family)   Your loving aunt, sister, sister-in-law and   (To MINTO.)   fellow guest - echoes those sentiments. A pleasant rest above all. Above all, that. A pleasant rest indeed!

(The family murmuring politely, go out. They file past the dining-room entrance before they disappear up the stairs. EMMA, still plainly in a fury, slams down the lid of the harpsichord and goes to pour herself another drink. MINTO is the last to leave the room.)

MINTO   Good night, my Lady.

EMMA   Minto, you stay.

MINTO   It is rather late.

EMMA   When have you ever found ten past eleven late?

MINTO   Well, I have some papers -

EMMA   Don't desert me in my distress. Oh! Minto, Minto! I know you think me a vulgar, drunken slut.

(Pause. MINTO, shrugging, decides to stay.)

MINTO   Whatever gave your Ladyship that idea?

EMMA   I don't give a fart for being thought what I am. But - if I'm vulgar it's not just because I'm a black-smith's daughter, but because I'm plain vulgar - and would be if I were the daughter of a duke - which, to a couple of Dukes I could mention, I almost have been - and God save us all from incestuous thoughts!

(Crosses and sits on chaise longue.)   Jesu Maria!
Do you think I couldn't have made myself into a
genteel English lady under old Sir Willum if I'd set
my mind to it? But God, who'd want to be as refined
as, say Kitty Matcham? What a death in life!
(She drinks.)   So - vulgar I always was, and
vulgar I'll always remain - and for choice. But slut?
What of that, Minto?

MINTO   Your Ladyship's generosity is known to be prodigious.
Why should it have stopped short of the bed?

EMMA   (thoughtfully)   Yes, I've been generous enough. I
didn't ever take money except in my 'teens. And old
Sir Willum - he had no cause for complaint. He
didn't want much - poor old love - although what with
my standing stark naked for hours on a plinth in
draughty rooms, while he - pottered about in his
special fashion - I caught a plaguy lot of colds. Poor
old Sir Willum! Well, I was an honest wife to him in
my own way.

(As MINTO raises his eyebrows.)

Oh, yes - that was Sir Willum's way too. Cuckolded
by England's greatest hero? It kept the old boy alive.
To be honest - a bit too long for propriety's sake. Oh,
what a boon we all were then to the cartoonists - with
Sir Willum beaming from a box at Drury Lane - and
me beside him, eight months gone with Horatia - and
Nelson on the other side, saluted from the stage with
music and drums and patriotic tableaux, and Tom
Tit tucked in there into the bargain -

MINTO   Where would she sit?

EMMA   Behind us, of course. She knew her place, even then.
But getting all the sympathy, the bitch! That gentle,
resigned look, that smile of infinite understanding and
forgiveness. Oh, I could have strangled her!
(After a pause.)   Get me another drink, love. It's
good for forgetting fear.

MINTO   (replenishing her tankard)   I might remind your

	Ladyship that it's also good for becoming drunk.
EMMA	Do you think I get drunker now than when we met five years ago?
MINTO	Your Ladyship has never seemed averse from fortifying by artificial aids a vivacity already richly endowed by nature.
EMMA	Jesus! (She takes a long drink.)
MINTO	(seriously) I think you drink more now, and get less drunk.
	(Pause.)
EMMA	Yes. You're a sharp one, Minto. Nothing much escapes you, does it? (Pause.) I'm scared of Hardy - and he knows it. (Striding about in sudden agitation.) I'm scared he's trying to shame Nelson into going out again himself. He's foxy, that Hardy. I fear that I might be sunk by Captain Hardy's hornpipe.
MINTO	(seriously) I don't think so.
EMMA	(eagerly) You don't? I still look well enough, do I?
MINTO	(politely) As desirable as when you sat for Romney.
EMMA	(sharply) Don't say that! I can eat flattery, God knows, but if you mention Romney, then I'll know you're lying.
MINTO	(quietly) I didn't say beautiful. I said desirable.
EMMA	By candle-light, to a man half-blind? (She dabs at her eyes.) Brandy tears.
MINTO	You must know that by candle-light or daylight, Nelson will always see you as Romney saw you - as his Divine Lady.
EMMA	But how do I see myself? Answer me that. When I get up in the mornings and look at myself in my glass, don't you think I don't say to myself - but he can't love that! Not that! It's too absurd. So

Francesca fills me up with a few tankards of porter
and brandy at breakfast, and by evening I'm the
Divine Lady again and I'm saying - but, of course
Nelson loves me, and he's damn lucky to have me.
But tonight's different, I don't know why.   (She
dabs her eyes again and puts the handkerchief away.)
Oh, my Nelson - I do love him!

MINTO   I think you do.

EMMA   Only think, Minto? By heaven, I love my Nelson
more than I love life.   (Catching herself in a
dramatic posture.)   No that's an Attitude and I
mustn't attitudinise about my feelings for Nelson.
Well, I suppose the truth is that I love Nelson
because he sees me in the only way I can ever bear
to be seen by any lover now -   (With sudden
anger.)   He's been in there long enough.   (She
goes to the harpsichord.)   Shall I see if my arts
still work?   (She opens the harpsichord and begins
to strum some notes again.)   We have a signal.
An absolute signal. He's never failed to answer it
yet. Mind you - after the way I've behaved tonight -
Well, we'll see.

(She plays the verse of Rule Britannia, not loudly
and heroically, but rather gently and prettily.
NELSON, in the dining-room, looks up, evidently
hearing. Then he goes back to work.)

I'm nervous.

(She continues to play but nothing appears to happen.
What in fact does happen is that NELSON walks
quickly out of the dining-room.)

(In alarm.)   Minto, did I behave so badly tonight
that he'll never forgive me?

(The question is answered for her as NELSON walks
in. EMMA rises from the harpsichord and goes to
NELSON. They kiss. MINTO goes out. EMMA
sinks gracefully on to one knee, bending her head in
submission.)

	Nelson, the culprit begs forgiveness.
NELSON	(trying to lift her) Emma, Emma –
EMMA	Oh, my Lord – I have most grievously offended, and I hereby submit myself to your Lordship's great will.
NELSON	(laughing at her) You know what my will is, Emma. Whether it's great is another matter – but it's unquenchable – that's certain.
EMMA	No – I must first have your gracious pardon and on my knee I beg it.
NELSON	Must we behave like this? There's no one here.
EMMA	(faintly irritated) I thought you'd like to see me on my knee before you, admitting my fault and craving humble indulgence.
NELSON	I like to see you in any position before me, but not now in an Attitude.
EMMA	You don't like my Attitudes?
NELSON	You know I adore them as I adore you – but not always, dearest Emma. Not when we are alone. (He kisses her passionately now – and she responds.)
EMMA	I was very bad, wasn't I?
NELSON	It's forgotten.
EMMA	Didn't I call him a bugger?
NELSON	Yes, but let us hope, inaccurately.
EMMA	I shamed you in front of all. Why do you put up with me?
NELSON	Don't you know why yet? (He kisses her greedily now, fondling her.)
EMMA	Have you finished talking to your Captains?
NELSON	Another five minutes.
EMMA	I'll go up straight.
NELSON	Please – (Embracing her.)

EMMA   I'll make it so good tonight –

NELSON   You don't need to make it anything but what it always
                is – and that is bliss enough.

EMMA   Who's attitudinising now?

NELSON   Oh, it's not an Attitude, my dearest, dearest heart.
                If you could only know the joy – the wonder – you see
                my hand is trembling –

EMMA   And that's not all. Come up very soon. When I do
                shame you, it's only out of love, and fear of losing
                you –

NELSON   How could you ever lose me?

                (GEORGE comes in from stairs.)

GEORGE   Oh. Excuse me.

NELSON   (still holding EMMA)   Come in, dear George.
                What is it?

GEORGE   I am leaving early in the morning and I want to thank
                you both for the most memorable four days of my
                life.

EMMA   (kissing him fondly)   Dearest George, I have loved
                having you as my guest at Merton and I promise I'll
                make sure that it won't be long before you return.

GEORGE   (bowing)   I am most grateful, my Lady.

EMMA   What's this my Lady again?

GEORGE   I'm sorry. Aunt Emma. May I speak to you, Uncle.

NELSON   Of course.

EMMA   (to NELSON)   Don't be long. And you tell your
                Captain Hardy I'm sorry for having called him a
                bugger –

                (Blowing a kiss to GEORGE she goes out. GEORGE,
                left alone with NELSON, is plainly nervous, but
                equally plainly conscious of a duty to be performed.
                NELSON is gazing after EMMA, hardly conscious of
                GEORGE. GEORGE fumbles in his pockets.)

GEORGE   I have this to give you, Uncle Horatio.   (He produces an object wrapped in paper.)

NELSON   What is it?

GEORGE   It's supposed to be against the ague. I was asked to give it to you by our maid at Bath.

NELSON   Very kind.

GEORGE   I told her you had hundreds of such things sent you through the post, but she insisted I give it to you personally and to be sure to tell you it came from our Betsy.

NELSON   (smiling)   I shall write to her tonight.

GEORGE   Oh, but you shouldn't bother –

NELSON   Of course I should.   Betsy – you say?

GEORGE   Yes.   But you shouldn't strain your eyes, Uncle – especially with writing letters that aren't important –

NELSON   Oh, but a letter of thanks for a kindly thought is important, George. Very important. Whatever they say of me, they mustn't ever say that I have forgotten my manners –

GEORGE   She'll be – I don't know what she'll be. I hope she doesn't sell it, that's all.

NELSON   Let her. But not for too small a price. You have been a most pleasant guest, George, and are growing into a fine young man. As her Ladyship says, you will always be welcome at Merton.

GEORGE   Thank you. There's just one other thing. You may be angry –

NELSON   With you? Never.

GEORGE   I've brought a letter to you from your wife.

(GEORGE takes it out of his pocket. NELSON makes no move to take it. There is a pause.)

NELSON   (quietly)   That you should never have done.

GEORGE   I gave a promise.

NELSON   That too, you should not have done. To whom did
                you give this promise?

GEORGE   To Aunt Frances.

NELSON   (angrily)   Don't call her that!   (Controlling
                himself.)   Where did you meet Lady Nelson?

GEORGE   In Bath, by accident.

NELSON   Where were your mother and father?

GEORGE   They had just gone on the London coach.

NELSON   And you were alone?

GEORGE   Yes.

NELSON   (bitterly)   By accident!   (He snatches the letter
                from GEORGE, but doesn't attempt to open it.)
                Very well. You've fulfilled your promise.   (He
                throws it unopened on to the harpsichord.)   And
                never make such a promise again.

GEORGE   No, Uncle Horatio.

NELSON   Well,   (Patting his shoulder.)   it's not you who
                are to blame, I suppose. Go to bed.

GEORGE   (getting letter)   There's just one thing else. I
                promised her you would read it.

                (Pause.)

NELSON   (with quiet rage)   How did you dare do that?

GEORGE   I didn't know how you felt, then. But I thought what-
                ever's happened, a husband can surely still read a
                letter from his wife. Especially you –

NELSON   Especially me?

GEORGE   Especially when the husband is you – of all people in
                the world.

NELSON   Thank you for the compliment, but this is a husband
                of all husbands in the world who happens to prefer to
                think his wife is no longer alive.   (Crosses to

above chaise longue.)

GEORGE   (crosses to him, with spirit)   But she is alive, isn't she, Uncle Horatio? As alive, anyway, as our maid Betsy.

(There is a pause. NELSON clenches and unclenches his fist, like a man whose patience is very strained. Then he abruptly picks up the letter, opens the covering, and pulls out the enclosure. He has only read a couple of sentences when he screws the letter up and hurls it to the floor.)

NELSON   (now in open rage)   You double-dealing, traitorous dog! I'll have you kicked out of this house tonight, and never come back!   (At the hall door, shouting.) Kitty! Kitty! Come here at once! And Matcham too! Come down!   (To GEORGE.)   I'll make you regret this trick you've played on me for the rest of your life –

GEORGE   But I played no trick, Uncle –

NELSON   To bring me back a letter of such vileness that I had to return it to her three years ago –

GEORGE   Vileness? How can you say that about it?

(KATHERINE has appeared breathlessly.)

KATHERINE   What is it, Horatio?

(NELSON ignores her. He is staring at the boy. MATCHAM, in a dressing-gown appears behind KATHERINE.)

NELSON   (to GEORGE)   You've read this letter?

GEORGE   Yes.

NELSON   She gave it to you to read?

GEORGE   She said I could – just to make sure it wasn't what you've just called it.   (Boldly.)   And it wasn't, it wasn't vile.

KATHERINE   (murmuring)   Don't – be impertinent.

(EMMA comes into the room, pushing aside the frightened MATCHAMS.)

EMMA   What's this?

NELSON   It has nothing to do with you, Emma.

EMMA   (crossing to him)   Nothing to do with me? You, shouting in a rage all over the house, and now shaking like you had the palsy - and it's nothing to do with me? Tell me this instant.

NELSON   I won't speak of it now - or probably ever. Just - take this boy away from me, please.

EMMA   (to KATHERINE)   What has he done?

KATHERINE   (murmuring unhappily)   I don't know - but I think he's brought some letter from Tom Tit -

EMMA   (appalled, to GEORGE)   Is that true?

(GEORGE is too distraught with what he seems to have done to NELSON to answer her.)

You answer me, then, Nelson. Is that true?

NELSON   I tell you - it is none of your business.

EMMA   (thunderstruck)   A secret letter from Tom Tit to you not my business?

NELSON   (raising his voice)   Leave me be. I must go out.

EMMA   Are you mad? You are certainly not going out in this weather, Nelson - and you are not leaving this room until I have a proper explanation.

MATCHAM   But Lady Hamilton is right. It's madness to go out in this weather.

NELSON   This is my house and not yet Lady Hamilton's, although she is sometimes pleased to think that it is otherwise. If I wish to leave it for my garden, I do so without her permission. Give me that lantern. (Coldly as EMMA still bars his way.)   By your leave, Lady Hamilton.

EMMA   (taking a step back)   Lady Hamilton?

(NELSON walks past her and goes out L. EMMA runs after him.)

Nelson!   (Then more pleadingly.)   Nelson –
Nelson.

(The lights fade to a complete blackout. During it we hear, at first, some music indicative of inner turmoil, and then the sound of wind and rain, inter- mingled at a moment by a peal of thunder. When the lights come on again it is to show the dining-room where HARDY, seated R. of table, still and wide- awake, and BLACKWOOD, seated at head of table asleep, are waiting. After several moments NELSON appears as from the front door. His cloak is now dripping wet. He makes his way quietly towards the stairs, sees candles still alight in the dining-room and goes towards it. HARDY stands up as NELSON enters.)

NELSON   (standing at the entrance)   I fear you have had a long watch.

HARDY   Oh, I had company.

(BLACKWOOD stumbles to his feet at the sound of NELSON's voice.)

BLACKWOOD   My Lord - you are s-s-safe returned?

(NELSON takes off his cloak and lays it across chair in U. L. corner of dining area. Smiling:)

NELSON   That safety can only be measured by the state of my health in the morning.

BLACKWOOD   Hardy and I - we l-l-looked everywhere for you.

NELSON   Didn't Hardy guess where I was?

HARDY   (to BLACKWOOD)   Captain Blackwood, it is time for your bunk. You leave for Portsmouth at dawn - which is in rather less than in two hours.

BLACKWOOD   Ay, ay, Captain.   (Bowing, naval fashion.)
Lord Nelson, I confess I am most h-h-heartily relieved to see you s-s-standing here before me. I

had so much f-feared - we had all so much f-feared -
Her Ladyship has even s-sent search parties out -

NELSON   (to HARDY)   Where is she?

HARDY   In bed at last.

NELSON   (to BLACKWOOD)   Good night, Captain Blackwood
                  - or what remains of this night. I am most sorry to
                  have disturbed the larger part of it.

BLACKWOOD   Oh, My Lord, that was n-n-nothing.   (Bowing.)
                  My Lord.   (He goes and we see him climbing
                  stairs to bed.)

HARDY   You should take a double tot of grog, I think.

                  (NELSON pours drinks from brandy on dining table.)

NELSON   (pretending to be outraged)   Grog, Hardy? My
                  best French brandy? But I suppose it would hardly
                  be called a hero's death to die of a chill contracted
                  on the roof of a folly in my garden, after a tiff with
                  my mistress.

HARDY   By all accounts it was something more than a tiff.

NELSON   Yes, it was, I suppose. Was there great uproar
                  afterwards?

HARDY   Not many turned in before three, I think. Her
                  Ladyship even later.

NELSON   (he pours another small glass)   Where is the boy?

HARDY   In his room.

NELSON   (anxiously)   And the letter? Did she read it?

HARDY   No. The boy has locked it up, and hidden the key.
                  There has been, as your Lordship might imagine,
                  something of a hue and cry.

NELSON   Has he talked?

HARDY   No.

NELSON   Not a word?

HARDY   Not that I know of.

NELSON	Not even that he read the letter himself?
HARDY	His mother heard him say that to you.
NELSON	Yes, I suppose she did. (Sits U.R. chair.) And she heard, and has no doubt informed you all, of his description of it - as the kind of letter that no honourable man would ever send back to his wife?
HARDY	Well - young eyes usually see the truth of things in a distorting mirror -
NELSON	But how is this truth distorted?
HARDY	How can I answer that without facts?
NELSON	You have the facts.
HARDY	(losing patience) I have the fact that you have wronged your wife. What you have never told me is how your wife has wronged you. I only know that she has.
NELSON	How do you know?
HARDY	Because I'm your friend and I know as a simple truth that you - Lord Nelson - could never behave as you have and as you do to that lady unless she had first done you some most grievous wrong. (After a pause.) She has, has she not?
NELSON	Yes.
HARDY	Most grievous?
NELSON	Yes.
HARDY	I don't ask how. I only ask, if the true facts are not known, how can the world pass true judgement?
NELSON	Oh Hardy, you don't understand the matter at all, do you?
HARDY	I said if I knew the true facts -
NELSON	(in mounting fury) You know the true facts. Six years ago, in Naples, I wittingly and of my own free will, deserted a loving and loyal wife for the embraces of a notorious charmer. How much did you

all laugh in the wardroom of the Vanguard when you
saw that happening? 'Not leaving his wife for that
woman', did you say? 'Not for the one who displayed
herself naked for show at fourteen in Vauxhall
Gardens, who was sold by Greville to Hamilton as
payment for a bad debt, and has been bedded by half
the nobility and gentry of England before becoming
Sir William's wife? Not leaving his wife for her!
Not for Emma Hamilton!' Do you think I never
imagined how loud that laughter must have been?

(Pause.)

HARDY
My Lord, the wardroom could not have guessed that
you were so aware. I did not guess it myself, until
this minute. You pretend very well, you see.

NELSON
Oh God, Hardy - how do you think I can keep my
sanity and not be aware?   (Pause. He turns his
face from HARDY.)   My Divine Lady? After an
insult to my King, don't you think I see exactly what
you see, a drunken, middle-aged woman making a
fool of herself and of me? Do you think I relish the
gutter-talk, don't wince at the vulgarity, and have
lost the capacity to smell liquor on the breath? Do
you think there isn't a moment in each day that I don't
feel blasted with shame?

(Pause.)

HARDY
Then why have you so long endured such days?

NELSON
(facing him)   Because after the days there are the
nights.

(Pause. NELSON smiles.)

HARDY
Does love begin and end in the bed, my Lord?

NELSON
I have found that in the release of the bed there lies
an ecstasy so strong and a satisfaction so profound
that it seems that it is everything that life can offer,
the very purpose of existence on earth - and when at
last I surrendered to Emma, I found - why should I
be ashamed to say it? - that carnal love concerns

the soul quite as much as it concerns the body. At least it does for me. You must understand that there is nothing in Emma I would change, Hardy. I want her exactly as she is - because I love her.

(Pause.)

HARDY

I don't think this love of yours does begin and end in the bed, my Lord.

NELSON

You are right. And yet without the bed what would it be? Nothing. But that other love - the tight brave smile, the rigid body, the - Oh, Hardy, that was a hell of humiliation - a hell - but a hell from which I am now so very happily escaped - (He covers his face. Then he rises, nods to HARDY and goes out to the stairs.) We should get some rest.

(HARDY follows him.)

HARDY

Did you say happily, my Lord?

NELSON

(continuing up the stairs) Find another word if you like. Satisfyingly?

HARDY

Is it so satisfying to be laughed at in Clarges Street?

(NELSON stops short.)

NELSON

That was nothing. A few brutish boors, probably hired by my enemies.

HARDY

Has your Lordship any enemies, apart from the French? I doubt if Napoleon would hire spies to risk jeering you into going out again to sea.

(NELSON turns violently and stares down at HARDY.)

NELSON

God damn you, Hardy, but you fight foul! (Looks down at him.) I'll not go out to Cadiz, do you hear?

HARDY

I hear.

(NELSON makes his way brusquely down the stairs and into the sitting-room. HARDY follows him.)

NELSON

(crossing room and sitting in chair D. L.) It's all you've thought about since that morning in Clarges

Street. 'I don't care how sacred a vow is', you've said, 'I don't care what it may cost him in spirit and health and love. I'll get him to go out again'. Well, Hardy, you won't and that's an end of it. Let them laugh and guffaw at me in the streets, and let them cheer Collingwood as their new hero –

HARDY   No. That they'll not do.

NELSON   Of course they will, when he wins his battle.

HARDY   He won't win it. Mind you, I don't say he'll lose it either. A couple of prizes, perhaps, and some damage to their flagship. Perhaps some damage to one or two of ours, but which must happen when two lines of warships sail in parallel, exchanging broadsides –

NELSON   In parallel? Are you mad? Go back to the dining-room and study my plan.

HARDY   I had many hours tonight to study it, my Lord. Laid out with all your silver, it looks very pretty.

NELSON   (rising and crossing to C.)   God damn it, Hardy, where in blazes on that table are two parallel lines of battle? Are you mad or drunk, sir? The two British lines of battle point at right angles to the enemy line, one at his heart, the other at his liver. The very genius of the plan is to reverse completely all the rules by which naval battles until now have been fought, and to abolish parallel lines altogether. This is annihilation, Hardy.

HARDY   (politely)   Yes, my Lord, I have often heard you say so.

NELSON   After this battle the French and Spanish fleets must never put to sea again. Not a single ship among them. God damn your eyes, Hardy, if my plan means anything at all, it means victory so complete and absolute that we will rule the seas and oceans for perhaps a hundred years –

HARDY   Oh yes, it is a very pretty plan.

NELSON   (crossing to HARDY, beside himself)   Pretty?
Pretty? By God, Hardy, if I had two arms I would
throttle you for that.

HARDY   I only meant that it looks pretty on your dining-table,
my Lord. I also meant that your dining-table was
not the Atlantic Ocean.

(Pause.)

NELSON   I've thought of everything, haven't I?

HARDY   Nearly everything.

NELSON   What have I left out?

HARDY   Yourself.

(Pause. NELSON laughs.)

NELSON   Do you think I can be caught by so foolish and
obvious a trap? Collingwood is a great commander.

HARDY   Not great. Say good –

NELSON   Good enough to win the battle with this plan.

HARDY   If he uses it.

NELSON   Why should he not use it? When I last saw him he
agreed to it in every detail –

HARDY   I've no doubt. But when, in a few weeks time, he
sees thirty or more French and Spanish sail, in
line of battle, on his horizon – and it will be quite an
awesome sight – five miles or more of broadsides
facing him and his outnumbered fleet, which does
your Lordship really believe he'll follow – your plan
or the training of a lifetime?

(Pause.)

NELSON   My plan.

HARDY   I trust you are right. Myself I believe that no
Admiral in the world would risk losing his entire
fleet in a single afternoon by following a revolution-
ary plan of battle, never tried before, and conceived
by a genius who has decided to be absent from the

action.

(NELSON is silent, unable to answer. The figure of
MINTO can be seen descending the stairs.)

Well, my Lord, have I your leave to go to bed? The
thought of it is infinitely inviting.

MINTO   I trust I don't interrupt?

NELSON   (sharply)   No, I think Captain Hardy has said all
he had to say.

HARDY   Lord Nelson.   Lord Minto.   (He exits upstairs.)

MINTO   I have a message for you.

NELSON   I can guess it.

MINTO   I have no doubt, my Lord, but may I satisfy my
conscience by delivering it.   Her Ladyship has just
paid me the delightful compliment of rousing me
from my sleep.   It appears that she heard your and
Hardy's voices on the stairs some moments ago.
They awakened her, in fact.

NELSON   (wearily)   And I am commanded to go to her at
once.

MINTO   No, my Lord.

NELSON   No?

MINTO   My message is the reverse.   Her Ladyship feels
herself so mortified by the events of tonight that she
has found herself in honour bound   (Yawning.)
forgive me - to lock and bolt the doors of her bedroom and she wishes me categorically to affirm that
no knock or entreaties, however loud and piteous,
will induce her to open them before mid-day
(Yawning again.)   - oh dear - when she has ordered
her carriage to take her on a round of visits to
various gentlemen with whom she feels she will be a
more welcome guest than under your Lordship's
roof.   Now I trust I have delivered her correctly.
I was particularly to remember the part about the
roof.   So, if your Lordship will forgive me, I will

return to my bed and pray to be allowed to sleep reasonably undisturbed by the ensuing commotions.

(MINTO exits upstairs. NELSON sits on chaise longue. After a pause GEORGE is seen creeping downstairs. He is carrying a bag.)

NELSON   (sharply)   Who is that? George? Come in here at once. Where are you going at this hour? You're not due to leave until eight –

GEORGE   Yes.

(Pause.)

NELSON   Where were you intending to walk to tonight?

GEORGE   London, I think.

NELSON   Nineteen miles, in the rain?

GEORGE   It's stopped raining.

NELSON   Give me that.   (He takes the bag and places it on floor.)   Sit down.

(GEORGE sits awkwardly on L. chair.)

You're running away?

(GEORGE nods.)

From me and Lady Hamilton? Well, that I understand. But why from your father and mother?

(GEORGE doesn't answer.)

Did you think you were going to be whipped?

GEORGE   I wouldn't have minded that.

NELSON   What is it then?

GEORGE   I want to leave this house, that's all.

NELSON   You are leaving this house, in three hours – with your parents.   (Crosses to table U.L. for drinks.)

GEORGE   I don't want them talking to me. They'll ask questions that I can't answer. Please, I don't want to talk to you either. May I go?

NELSON	No. (He pours out a glass of wine and crosses to GEORGE.) You look as if you'd been crying. Have you?
GEORGE	Not much.
NELSON	You'd better drink this.
GEORGE	I don't want it.
NELSON	It'll make you feel better.
GEORGE	Nothing will make me feel better. Nothing as long as I live.
NELSON	Drink it.

(GEORGE takes it obediently, sips a mouthful and hands it back hastily.)

George, whatever it was I said that upset you, you must forget it.

GEORGE	I'll try. May I go?
NELSON	(pointing to the bag) You still have that letter?
GEORGE	Yes.
NELSON	You're going to return it to her?
GEORGE	No, of course not. If I see her I'll just say I delivered it, as I promised, and that you read it.
NELSON	And called it vile?
GEORGE	No, never.
NELSON	Why are you keeping it?
GEORGE	To read again.
NELSON	Why?
GEORGE	I might understand.
NELSON	Might you? I don't think you will.
GEORGE	Nor do I.
NELSON	Will you promise never to show it to anyone else in the world?

GEORGE

What kind of person do you think I am?

(Pause. NELSON pours himself another brandy.)

NELSON

A very good, brave and most honourable boy. A nephew I am proud to have.

(GEORGE makes a sound.)

Don't laugh. Too many people laugh at me these days. Despise me, if you like, but don't laugh. What I just said was true.   (He finishes the brandy, and faces GEORGE.)   Very well, George. Here it is. '16 Somerset Street.'   (Quietly and without the faintest effort of memory.)   'The eighteenth of December eighteen-hundred and one. My dearest husband, it is some time that I have written to you. The silence you have imposed is more than my affection will allow me –

(GEORGE stares at him with wide eyes.)

and in this instance I hope you will forgive me for not obeying you. One thing I omitted in my letter of July which I now have to offer for your accommodation – a comfortable warm house.'

(GEORGE, understanding that NELSON has not only read the letter, but in fact knows it by heart, drops his head in misery.)

(Continuing gently and remorselessly.)   'Do, my dear husband, let us live together. I can never be happy until such an event takes place. I assure you again, I have but one wish in the world, to please you. Let everything be buried in oblivion, it will pass away like a dream.'

(GEORGE makes a gesture for him to stop.)

Hear it out. A few more tears tonight won't hurt. 'I can only entreat you to believe I am most sincerely and affectionately your wife, Frances H. Nelson.' You see that you and she need have had no fears that I didn't read it.

GEORGE	(at length) And sent it back - with that message?
NELSON	(nodding) I, of all people in the world -
GEORGE	What did she do to you to make you do that? It must have been something really dreadful -
NELSON	It was.
GEORGE	What was it?
NELSON	She wrote me that letter.
	(Pause.)
GEORGE	But it's a kind and loving letter.
NELSON	It's brutal -
GEORGE	It isn't -
NELSON	Many brutal acts are done out of love and kindness, George. Perhaps most. (Seeing his blank face.) Oh dear, must I explain? Is this so important to you? (Crosses to above chaise longue.)
GEORGE	(simply) The most important thing on earth.
NELSON	It won't save my honour, which you seem so to cherish.
GEORGE	If it's true, it will.
NELSON	It's true. George, when one has done wrong to someone - and open wrong, a shameful and humiliating wrong, a wrong on an epic scale, to be forgiven for it is the very hell.

(GEORGE stares at him in silence.)

I shock you, of course. You're my Reverend father's grandson and to answer forgiveness by hatred must seem unchristian at the least. But is it? Jesus told us how to answer a blow on the cheek, but he never told us how to answer a kiss. I haven't always been a bad Christian, George. I've even managed sometimes, to love my enemies a little. Not too much, mind you. Moderation in all things. But I do try to save them from drowning, even at

risk to our ships, and no one can say I ever treated
a prisoner-of-war other than with honour and
gentleness. But, George –

(He seems to find it hard to continue. GEORGE's
eyes are unwaveringly fixed on his, and they are the
eyes of his own conscience.)

George – what about an enemy who won't retaliate?
Who answers every broadside with a signal gently
fluttering at the mast which says: 'Whatever you do
to me, my dearest husband, I will always forgive
you and go on loving you for ever. ' What about that
enemy, George? What is there, then, left for me,
but to hate? Have you understood even a little?

GEORGE   No.

NELSON   Well, you're in good company. Go back to your
room, now. No more of this nonsense of running
away. It's cowardly to run away, didn't you know
that?   (GEORGE nods.)   Well, then, back to
your bed. Good night, George.

(GEORGE continues on his way for a few steps
before stopping.)

GEORGE   Good night – Uncle Horatio.   (He continues to go
up.)   Thank you for the port.

(NELSON turns quickly and goes into the dining-room
a deeply distressed man and sits on chair at head of
table. It is some time before he has recovered
himself enough to rest his head on his hand out-
stretched on the table – no longer ague-ridden and
sobbing, but utterly exhausted.

After a few moments EMMA appears at the head of
the staircase. She is in a peignoir. She comes down
the stairs with extreme timidity – at one moment
even apparently considering a return to her room.
Then she makes up her mind and walks to the dining-
room entrance. She looks at NELSON for a moment
then slides into the chair L. of his, and rests her
head on his shoulder.)

EMMA   Oh, Nelson, forgive me!

                (NELSON looks up. For a moment he seems so
                dazed as not to take in her presence.)

NELSON   (at length)   For what, my dearest?

EMMA   For whatever I did.

NELSON   What was it?

EMMA   I thought you'd tell me.

NELSON   I can't, Emma. I don't know.

EMMA   I expect you'll remember. And I'm sure it was
                something dreadful I did to you.

NELSON   You did nothing dreadful to me, my dearest. You
                never have and you never could.   (Feeling her
                hand.)   You're cold.

EMMA   Sleeping alone can freeze a lady –

NELSON   Well – that at least can be rectified.

                (He gets up and stretches himself. EMMA puts her
                head on his breast again, lovingly and timidly.)

EMMA   I've been so scared.

NELSON   What of?

EMMA   That you'd left me.

NELSON   I'll never leave you, Emma. Not until death.

EMMA   Have you been drinking brandy?

NELSON   Rather a lot, it seems.

EMMA   Learning from me, eh?

NELSON   I haven't quite your own regal capacity for the stuff.

EMMA   (holding up the decanter)   Well, you're not doing
                too badly for a beginner. Shall we have one now?
                Together.

NELSON   Why not?

                (EMMA pours for both.)

EMMA	What shall we drink to?
NELSON	To Emma - and her Nelson. What else? (Drinks.)
	(NELSON looks down at the plan, and with a brusque gesture disarranges it suddenly from a neat pattern to chaos.)
EMMA	You've spoiled your pretty plan.
NELSON	Yes. Did you too think it pretty? (Crosses U.L. of EMMA.)
EMMA	Very pretty - and I'd have kept this table laid out just this way - to show to visitors exactly how Nelson won his battle off Cadiz.
NELSON	(gently) Exactly how Collingwood won Nelson's battle off Cadiz.
EMMA	I said how Nelson won it. (Pause.)
NELSON	Emma - I have not asked you -
EMMA	No, but you were going to.
NELSON	No, my dearest, you are wrong. (Sits down again at head of table.) I would never, never have asked.
EMMA	But you might have called me 'Lady Hamilton' a little more, and shown a greater fancy for going out alone in the rain as the time of Collingwood's battle approached? I love my Nelson - but I love all of him. I don't want him only half a man, with the better half pining to be out at sea.
NELSON	Has Hardy talked with you tonight?
EMMA	That bugger? I wouldn't soil my lips.
NELSON	(embracing her) Oh, Emma, my darling!
EMMA	It wasn't only that thought, Nelson - to be really truthful -
NELSON	You always are really truthful.
EMMA	Well, I can exaggerate a bit, like paying a round of visits to various gentlemen. (They both laugh,

holding hands.) I wouldn't want to be thought of as a woman who kept you from going out when the country needed you. It is my country, too, you know.

NELSON You, too, think I'm needed?

EMMA There's only one Nelson in the world. But he's mine. Mine alone.

NELSON Truly only yours.

EMMA Mine to keep - and mine to give too. (She is near tears.) Only - one thing, my darling - this time take care. (She can't go on.)

NELSON Yes, my heart.

EMMA Don't leave your Emma alone and deserted.

NELSON I won't.

EMMA Swear it properly. Swear that this time you'll do all that lies in your power, not to get yourself killed.

NELSON (gravely) I will do all that lies in my power not to leave my Emma alone and deserted, and that I do most solemnly swear to, before God.

EMMA Well, you're good with vows, and you do your best to keep them. You'd have kept the one about not going out, you say?

NELSON (kissing her hand) Yes, I do. Oh, my Emma, I love you so deeply.

EMMA (getting up) No, Nelson. That won't do at all. I want something more memorable. Something I can quote to my friends. I've thought of something -

NELSON I would expect that you might have.

EMMA I wrote it down in my journal in bed.

(As NELSON looks at her.)

Oh yes. You didn't need to risk any agues in a wet garden. I'd have told you this in bed - but I wanted you to know I was giving you - not having you filched from me by an underhand, contriving prick of a

	Flag-Captain. Now let me remember. I know. 'Dear Emma, brave Emma. If there were more Emmas in the world there'd be more Nelsons.' How do you like that?
NELSON	(staring at her) I like it very much. I like it because it's absolutely true.
EMMA	Not really. Nelsons are born, not made.
NELSON	They can sometimes be reborn. (He begins to arrange the table again.) My pretty battle. Well, we shall see.
EMMA	(watching him) Just tell me one thing, love, it will be another victory, won't it?
NELSON	I think so.
EMMA	A big one?
NELSON	Yes. Very big.
EMMA	It has to be big, my darling, because, since the crowds in the streets have taken to laughing at us –
NELSON	Laughing?
EMMA	You heard them in Clarges Street.
NELSON	I heard nothing but cheers.
EMMA	(holding his arms) You heard laughter and you knew who it was they laughed at. Well, I am grown a little laughable, I suppose, these days. I should fast a little, take off weight. And drink less, of course.
	(Absent-mindedly, she takes a gulp of brandy. NELSON smiles affectionately. She takes his hand.)
	Oh my darling, to afford an Emma Hamilton, you need a very big victory indeed. Then you'll find they won't laugh any more. (Picking up two sauce-boats.) What are these?
NELSON	The lead ships of our two attacking lines –
EMMA	One of them now the Victory, I suppose?

NELSON   Well, it may be.

EMMA   And now with you in it.

NELSON   It will be my flagship, Emma.

EMMA   (accusingly)   But, how often, at this table, have I
                heard you say that this one - the Victory   (She
                flourishes the sauce-boat.)   will have to bear so
                heavy a weight of enemy broadsides for the best part
                of an hour from at least five of their biggest
                battleships.   (Crosses to above chair U. L. of
                table.)

NELSON   Well, perhaps only four.

EMMA   Holy Jesus, isn't four enough? And with you
                strutting about on your quarter deck with all those
                stars and medals blazing like the sun.

NELSON   I don't strut, Emma.

EMMA   Why do you have to be in the Victory?

NELSON   (smoothly)   But I don't have to be in the Victory.
                I recommended to Collingwood to fly his flag in a
                frigate somewhere to the rear - the better to control
                the action.

EMMA   Oh yes! I can just see you flying your flag in a
                frigate - somewhere to the rear!

NELSON   There's no shame in that.

EMMA   (near tears again)   No shame to Collingwood,
                perhaps. But your flag? Oh, Nelson, you do lie to
                me sometimes! Do you remember what you have
                just vowed to me?

NELSON   Very clearly.

EMMA   Then vow another one. Vow about this.   (She
                picks up a sauce-boat, and puts it carefully to the
                rear.)

NELSON   Two vows in one morning is a little too much for the
                Almighty, don't you think? Especially when the one
                will so absolutely cover the other.

EMMA   Will it?   (Embracing him.)   Then leave your
                battle for tonight. Let's go up. Time's short. Now
                do you remember your little speech?

                (She goes to the entrance. He replaces the sauce-
                boat exactly where it was. EMMA has reached the
                stairs.)

NELSON   My little speech? Oh yes.

                (He goes. She is waiting for him.)

                Now, let me see. Brave, dear Emma.

EMMA   No, no, no! It's 'dear Emma, brave Emma –

NELSON   Dear Emma, brave Emma. If there were more
                Emmas – oh dear, I forget what would happen –

EMMA   There'd be more Nelsons.

NELSON   May the great God, whom I worship, grant to my
                country – and for the benefit of Europe in general,
                a great and glorious victory; and may no misconduct
                in anyone tarnish it; and may humanity after victory
                be the predominant feature in the British fleet. For
                myself, individually, I commit my life to Him who
                made me, and may His blessing light upon my
                endeavours for serving my country faithfully. To
                Him I resign myself and the just cause which is
                entrusted to me to defend. Amen, amen, amen.

                (The lights fade quickly but remain on the Turner-
                esque backcloth, while the gunfire grows even
                louder. Then, through the gunfire we hear the single
                tolling of a church bell. The lights on the backcloth
                fade quickly and the gunfire rumbles into silence.
                There is the sound of church music.
                When the lights go on we are in Merton.   LADY
                NELSON, in deep mourning, is standing very still in
                the sitting-room. The furniture is covered with
                dust sheets. FRANCESCA, in deep distress, comes
                down the stairs.)

FRANCESCA   Lady Hamilton, vi vuole vedere, eccellenza, ma
                forse sarebbe –

(As FRANCES appears not to understand.)

Lady Hamilton - not good - not well - is better - you come back another day.

FRANCES   Well, perhaps if I could leave her a note?

(EMMA can be seen walking, none too steadily, towards the hall area. She is in a nightdress, and is trying unsuccessfully to put on the purple mantle she wore as Andromache.)

EMMA   (off)   Francesca! Francesca! Dove stai, idiota?

(FRANCES moves to D. L. of harpsichord. FRANCESCA flies up the stairs to mask FRANCES from EMMA.)

FRANCESCA   Se n'e andata - se n'e andatornate a letto.

EMMA   L'ho vista, bugiarda. Her carriage is still outside.

(She pushes FRANCESCA out of the way and goes into the sitting-room where FRANCES has risen to greet her. The bell tolls.)

Lady Nelson.   (She curtsies clumsily.)

FRANCES   Lady Hamilton.   (She returns the curtsey with dignity.)

(EMMA indicates the mantle. FRANCESCA, near tears, drapes it round her. The bell tolls again.)

EMMA   (meanwhile to FRANCES)   I've been through my whole wardrobe and found nothing else of mourning.

(FRANCESCA goes.)

Purple is mourning, isn't it? Anyway it was for Andromache.

(The bell tolls.)

Your visit, Lady Nelson, does me great honour. To what do I attrib - attribute it?

FRANCES   (crossing to EMMA)   I have news of the greatest importance for yourself, and I judged it best that I

should be the one to give it you, rather than that you
read it in the newspapers tomorrow.

(The bell tolls again.)

EMMA   I don't read the newspapers any more. Sit down,
                    Lady Nelson.   (She looks around.)   There
                    should be some refreshment for your Ladyship.
                    (Crosses up to table.)

FRANCES   Please. I don't need any refreshment.

EMMA   Well, this Ladyship does. Excuse me.   (She takes
                    up a bottle of brandy from the table and slops some
                    into a tankard.)   Your Ladyship should see the
                    dining-room before you leave. It is left exactly as he
                    arranged it one night to show the two fleets as they
                    were to come into action - and as they did come into
                    action - almost exactly so, from all accounts -
                    (She drinks again. The bell tolls.)

                    (Suddenly screaming.)   Oh why don't they stop that
                    bell? We all know Nelson's dead! Wasn't it a
                    victory? The biggest   (Her voice breaks.)   yet
                    - as he vowed it would be. Forgive me, your
                    Ladyship. My legs are rather weak from staying in
                    bed.   (Sits on floor C.)

FRANCES   It was wrong of me to come. I see that now.

EMMA   Why? You've come to gloat, haven't you?

FRANCES   No, no. That's not true. Simply not true.

EMMA   If I'd been in your shoes, I'd have come down here to
                    gloat.

FRANCES   No. I am sure you would not, Lady Hamilton.

EMMA   Oh yes I would - because that's the kind of woman I
                    am.

FRANCES   I don't believe it. But there is nothing that I have
                    learnt of you that has ever indicated anything but a
                    most wide and generous nature.

                    (Pause. EMMA laughs.)

EMMA Oh God, how easy are words!

FRANCES My husband left my bed for yours. He was bound to have left it, one day, for somebody's. I have understood that - for a long time now. Why need we quarrel because the bed happened to be yours?

EMMA We quarrel because you were my enemy. You hated me, didn't you?

FRANCES (quietly) Yes, I did.

EMMA You were there, waiting. Always waiting.

FRANCES I was waiting for his old age.

  (Pause.)

EMMA (raising her glass) Oh well. Here's to his old age, then! (She drinks.)

FRANCES (rising and crossing to EMMA's R.) Lady Hamilton, a document has arrived, signed by Lord Nelson, and duly attested. It is the last known testament of my - of Lord Nelson's - life, and it leaves you, Emma, Lady Hamilton, as a bequest to the nation.

  (There is a long pause. The bell tolls. Then EMMA throws her head back and literally shouts with laughter.)

EMMA A bequest to the nation? Me? Oh God in Heaven! I think I'll die of this. (She continues to laugh in high hysterics watched with deep concern by FRANCES.) Left to the nation? Me, on a plinth in Westminster Hall. Oh, my poor, poor Nelson! What a baby he was!

  (The bell tolls.)

FRANCES Everything possible will be done to see that my Lord's last wish is met. The Earl himself has agreed -

EMMA The Earl? What Earl?

FRANCES Earl Nelson - William Nelson that was, my

	husband's brother.
EMMA	So he's an Earl now, is he? The arse-licking Dean. And what have the rest of that grubby crew of Nelson's got? William's son - he'll be something -
FRANCES	The Viscount Trafalgar.
EMMA	The Viscount Trafalgar. That little snotty-nosed brat? Oh God, what a world! And my child? His and mine?
	(The bell tolls.)
	And I suppose they're all back your way now? Well, quite a triumph for you, isn't it?
FRANCES	You don't understand me, Lady Hamilton.
	(Pause.)
EMMA	No. I never did. I never understood you at all, I suppose.
	(The bell tolls. EMMA comes close to FRANCES and stares at her.)
	I wonder what it's like to be good.
FRANCES	Trying to be is not always very easy.
EMMA	Did you ever understand me?
FRANCES	No.
EMMA	It's a funny world, isn't it?
FRANCES	I think you should go back to bed, and I'll say goodbye. I will do everything in my power to see that your debts at least are paid for by Parliament.
EMMA	Parliament? (Laughing.) They won't even put it to the vote. (Looking at her mantle.) Oh withered is the garland of war. Young boys and girls - I can't remember, what young boys and girls did. The usual, I suppose. (To FRANCES.) I can only remember - the odds is gone, and there is nothing left remarkable beneath the visiting moon. It was good of you to come, Lady Nelson.

FRANCES   Lady Hamilton.   (She exits.)

EMMA   (crosses to harpsichord and closes lid)   Funny
world.

(Stands and exits up stairs.)

CURTAIN

FURNITURE AND PROPERTY PLOT

ACT ONE
Scene 1

Set (L. side of stage):
  U.C. Two chairs
          Table
          Tray of coffee (4 cups)
  U.L. Bench
          On floor
          Large travelling bag
          Hatbox
  D.L. Sofa
          On floor
          Small case

Personal:
  BETSY   Hatbox
             KATHERINE's
               travelling coat
  GEORGE Books
  FRANCES Reticule
             In it
               Letter
               Purse

ACT ONE
Scene 2

Set (U.R. corner of stage):
  U.R. Two chairs
          Large desk
           On it
             COLLINGWOOD's
               despatch
             Admiralty's testimonial
             Workpapers, etc.
             Blotter
             Pens
             Ink

ACT ONE
Scene 3

Set
In Bedroom area R.
  D.R. Large bed
          On it
          Several pillows
  R.   Bedside table
  U.R. Dressing-table
          On it
          Large mirror
          Candlestick
          Perfume bottles
          Cosmetics
          Hand mirror
          Comb
          Vanity box
            containing
            make-up
  U.R. Screen masking
          powder room

  U.C. Chair
          On it
          EMMA's peignoir

In boudoir area L.
  D.C. Table
          Two chairs
  U.C. Chair
  U.L. Above fireplace
          Portrait of EMMA
  L.   Table
          On it
          Candlesticks
          Glasses
          Drink
           Gin
           Brandy
           Wine

Offstage
  In powder room
    Tankard   )
    Porter   )
    Green dress) FRANCESCA
    Flask   )
    Reticule   EMMA

ACT TWO

Set
  In dining area R.
    D.R. Armchair
    R.   Dining-room table
            Round it
              Four chairs
            On it
              Map
              Candles
              Decanter of brandy
              Silver   ) arranged as
              Glasses   ) NELSON's
              Sauceboats) battle plan
    U.C. Armchair

  In drawing-room area L.
    D.C. Chaise longue
    U.L. On wall
            EMMA's portrait
          Table
            On it
              Dagger
              Glasses
              Tankard
              Drinks
                Champagne
                Brandy
                Wine
                Sherry
                Gin
                Rum

Harpsichord
  On it
    Sheet music
    for
      KATHER-
      INE
    EMMA's
    stole
  Stool
  L.   Two chairs
  D.L. Large arm-
          chair

Offstage
  Upstairs
    Bag   GEORGE

Personal
  GEORGE Letter
          BETSY's
          present

During second black-
  out
    Cover all furniture
    except drawing-
    room table with
    dustsheets

    Check:
      Brandy and
      tankard on table